AF469742

BP PORTRAIT AWARD 2019

National Portrait Gallery

Published in Great Britain by
National Portrait Gallery Publications
National Portrait Gallery
St Martin's Place, London WC2H 0HE

Published to accompany the BP Portrait Award 2019,
held at the National Portrait Gallery, London,
from 13 June to 20 October 2019, Scottish National
Portrait Gallery, Edinburgh, from 7 December 2019 to
22 March 2020 and Ulster Museum, Belfast, from April
to June 2020.

For a complete catalogue of our current publications
please visit our website at www.npg.org.uk/publications

Copyright © National Portrait Gallery 2019

Text on pages 10–18 courtesy Christopher Baker.

Adapted extract from exhibition leaflet on page 78
courtesy Tony Wheeler.

The moral rights of the authors have been asserted.
All rights reserved. No part of this publication may be
reproduced, stored in a retrieval system or transmitted
in any form or by any means, whether electronic or
mechanical, including photocopying, recording
or otherwise, without the prior permission in writing of
the publisher.

ISBN 978 1 85514 707 2

A catalogue of this book is available
from the British Library.

10 9 8 7 6 5 4 3 2 1

Head of Commercial: Anna Starling
Publishing Manager: Kara Green
Project Editor: Tijana Todorinovic
Design: Richard Ardagh Studio
Production: Ruth Müller-Wirth
Photography: Prudence Cuming Associates
Printed and bound in Belgium
Cover: *Manresa* by Frances Borden

Every purchase supports the
National Portrait Gallery, London

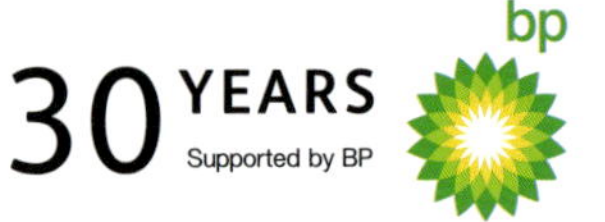

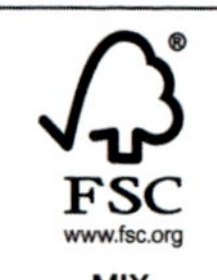

CONTENTS

Each year, the BP Portrait Award exhibition showcases exceptional works of contemporary painted portraiture and this year's exhibition, which marks thirty years of BP sponsorship, is no different. With the removal of the age limit in 2007 and the opening up of the competition to artists worldwide, the number of submissions has increased exponentially. It has become one of the most prestigious prizes internationally in contemporary portraiture and the works selected for exhibition together represent some of the best examples of the genre.

This year, the final forty-four exhibited works were selected from a total of 2,538 entries, from eighty-four countries, submitted to the competition. As the works were considered anonymously, my fellow judges and I assessed the paintings in terms of their technique, quality and what they disclose of the artist's own approach to the subject and how this resonates with the viewer. Often, the majority of works entered into the competition depict 'ordinary' people rather than celebrity or society figures, encouraging the democratisation of contemporary portraiture.

My congratulations to this year's four prizewinners for their exceptional and inspiring works. The First Prize for this year's competition has been awarded to Charlie Schaffer for his portrait *Imara in Her Winter Coat*. This year's Second and Third Prizes have been awarded to Carl-Martin Sandvold and Massimiliano Pironti respectively, and the BP Young Artist Award prizewinner is Emma Hopkins.

The Award aims to continue to inspire both artists who submit works into the competition and those visiting the exhibition. Each year, the Travel Award offers exhibiting artists the opportunity to produce portraits that are inextricably linked to the location in which they have been made. Additionally, the BP Next Generation workshops will provide inspiration for younger artists developing their portrait-making practice.

At the National Portrait Gallery, we would like to extend our gratitude to BP for their continued support of the exhibition programme, which has inspired and engaged an ever-growing number of artists creating works of painted portraiture. My sincere thanks go to Bob Dudley and his team, and in particular to Dev Sanyal, Peter Mather and Des Violaris, for their commitment to the success of this partnership.

Nicholas Cullinan
Director, National Portrait Gallery

SPONSOR'S FOREWORD

At BP, we look to build long-term partnerships and we are really proud to have supported the National Portrait Gallery, London, and this internationally acclaimed competition for thirty years. Several significant connections come to mind as I reflect on this milestone.

The first is that we are both British-based organizations with a global reach and outlook. Over the past three decades, together we have encouraged tens of thousands of artists from countries throughout the world to submit their work to this renowned competition for international portrait painters.

A second connection is our shared commitment to enabling more people to experience the very best of arts and culture. The quality of work is always of the highest standard and more than five million people have visited the annual exhibition since 1990, either at the National Portrait Gallery in London or elsewhere across the UK.

The third connection is a personal one for me. I am always fascinated by the human stories behind the paintings and I believe this is what makes the BP Portrait Award so enduringly popular. As well as admiring the different styles and techniques employed, we are drawn to consider what each portrait can tell us about the artist, the sitter and the relationship between the two.

On behalf of BP, I'd like to thank every artist who has participated in the Award over the past thirty years, including those who have submitted 2,538 entries from eighty-four countries this year. I'd also like to applaud the expertise and commitment of the judges in selecting the winning entries and exhibited portraits for this year's competition.

In a world that is moving ever-faster with even more demands on our time, it is a real pleasure to pause and enjoy the exceptional quality of such diverse contemporary portraits from so many talented artists.

Finally, I'd like to thank Nicholas Cullinan, Pim Baxter and their team at the National Portrait Gallery for our continued partnership and congratulate them all for delivering one of the longest-running arts competitions in the world. I hope that every visitor, new or returning, will enjoy this exhibition and many more to come.

Bob Dudley
Chief Executive, BP

A QUESTION OF RECOGNITION

Christopher Baker

Christopher Baker is Director of
European and Scottish Art and
Portraiture for the National Galleries
of Scotland. He was a judge of the
BP Portrait Award in 2016. This year's
exhibition will be shown at the
Scottish National Portrait Gallery
from December 2019.

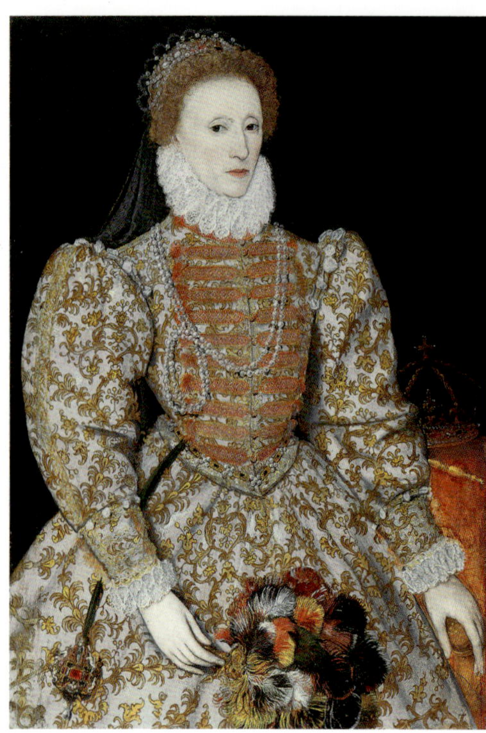

Queen Elizabeth I (1533–1603)
by an unknown continental
artist, c.1575 (NPG 2082)
Oil on panel, 1130 × 787mm

One of the challenges encountered by a portrait painter is to bring a quality of immediacy and conviction to their work – to convey the spark of life that is unique to their subject and forge a link between it and the viewer's experience. Many of the entries to the BP Portrait Award undoubtedly achieve precisely this effect and the result is what makes their paintings so compelling and popular. The element of vitality, combined with technical skill, is a key reason why a portrait might be judged as appropriate for inclusion in the exhibition. In the majority of cases, though, the issue of likeness

– how reliable or accurate or indeed typical the representation is – cannot be considered simply because most of the subjects in the exhibition are not well-known figures familiar through other forms of representation, but instead are the friends, relatives or members of the community of the painter.

Consequently, it might be argued that the judging has a purity about it, as it is the art, artifice and emotive force of the painting that is being weighed without reference to other images of the sitter in your mind's eye or knowledge of their

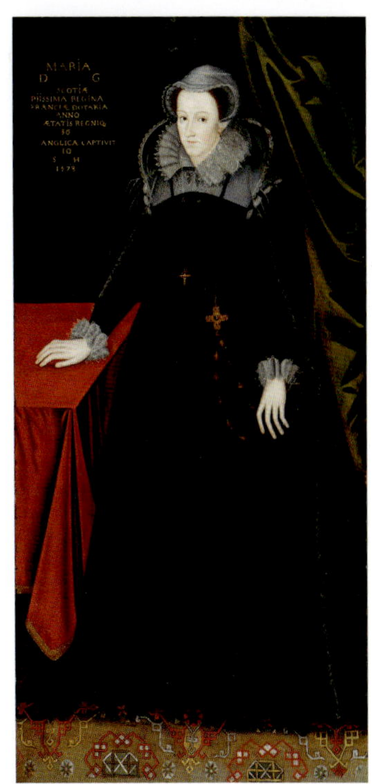

Mary Queen of Scots (1542–87)
by an unknown artist, c.1610–15
(National Galleries of Scotland,
PG 1073)
Oil on canvas, 2015 × 957mm

world and reputations. I was fortunate
to be a member of the jury a couple
of years ago and at the time I was
struck not only by the sense of
liberation this allowed but also by the
concentration it encouraged.

It is perhaps worth stepping back and
thinking about the resonance of such
a process in the context of the
National Portrait Galleries in London
and Edinburgh, two of the venues
where the exhibition will be shown in
the competition's thirtieth anniversary
year of BP sponsorship. Such galleries
are chiefly defined by famous faces.
This quality has a strong sense of

reassurance about it; it's pleasing to
know that in the National Portrait
Gallery in London you will find and
can have an intimate encounter with
William Shakespeare or Elizabeth I,
while in Edinburgh, Robert Burns and
Mary Queen of Scots are patiently
waiting for your attention.

Both founded in the nineteenth
century, these institutions were
conceived to celebrate
achievement and eminence
through portraiture at a time when
definitions of who might be
included were relatively narrow by
modern standards. The breadth of

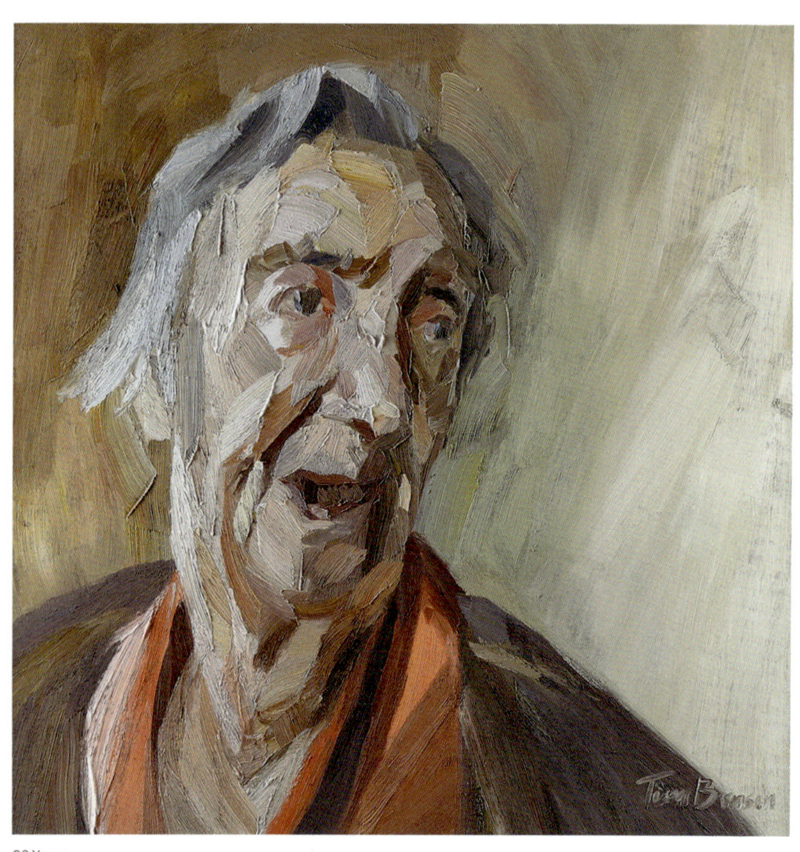

92 Years
by Tim Benson, 2011
Oil on canvas, 1200 × 1220mm

their collections has quite rightly exploded in recent decades to encompass the full and evolving diversity of achievement across contemporary society. For the National Portrait Gallery, London, the key moment of transition came in 1969 when it started collecting portraits of living subjects (previously, with the sole exception of royalty, sitters had to have been deceased for a decade before being admitted). North of the border, the same change arrived in the early 1980s when commissions started to be made by the Scottish National Portrait Gallery. These changes mean that now in both buildings historical figures, royalty and literary greats rub shoulders with (or hang close to) living politicians, scientists, entrepreneurs, giants of sport and fashion icons, as well as stars of the music and film industries. The quality of the portraiture acquired or commissioned is of course a key consideration, but it is underpinned by the appeal of recognition, at least of the name and reputation of the sitter, if not their face.

The BP Portrait Award sometimes features well-known sitters, but at the same time it encourages and sets up a nationwide conversation about the art of portraiture more generally and the status of painting in particular, rather than how famous figures might best be represented. In an age of celebrity, which is fuelled by media intrusion and results in us being oversaturated with images of figures in public life, this is especially appealing.

The exhibition also thrives because of recognition of a different kind, which has nothing to do with fame. The portraits allow viewers to connect with more universal experiences and concerns as the subjects painted are wonderfully various and every now and then we may see something of ourselves in or through them – old, young, joyous, glum, confident, angst-ridden, remote, intimate, healthy, frail, urban, rural and from all around the world. Such a list of attributes with which we can identify could be extended exponentially.

These democratic and expansive qualities which characterise the Award have over the last three decades mirrored broader changes in the status and role of portrait galleries. Allowing depictions of living subjects to be acquired was a fundamental change of direction, and over the same period they have also become more welcoming, social and noisy spaces, international in outlook and sensitive to the expectations and needs of their visitors, where issues around identity are highlighted.

The question of noise is especially interesting, as delightfully the BP Portrait Award exhibition often stimulates a great deal of discussion. It prompts a buzz of debate among visitors, who in the company of contemporary portraits feel emboldened to take on the role of critics, either expressing their approval or disputing the decisions of the judges about which works have received prizes. I've listened in on some of these impromptu discussions and debate often also rages about the range of styles of portraits on display and their relative merits – from the gestural and painterly, which privilege the medium employed and revel in its use, as in Tim Benson's *92 Years* (exhibited in the BP Portrait Award 2012), to the meticulous and photorealistic, like *Bertha* by Jesús María Sáez de Vicuña Ochoa (exhibited in the BP Portrait Award 2018), in which the process is almost hidden in order to inspire awe of a different sort.

The contrasts between such approaches can be explored and highlighted through the way in which the exhibition is installed. From a curatorial perspective, it

has always been one of the great pleasures of the exhibition to create interesting groupings of portraits in order to enrich the experience of the viewer and establish visual dialogues. It is probably true to say that the vast majority of those who come and enjoy such conversations in front of the paintings are not likely to have the opportunity to sit for a painted portrait themselves, but this certainly does not stop them considering the interesting question of how they might like to be portrayed given such an opportunity and in view of the amazing array of possibilities laid out in the exhibition – this is also an area where trenchant views are expressed.

Another facet of the Award that is enthusiastically discussed is its increasingly international nature, which is especially fascinating and seems to show no sign of stopping – last year, submissions were received from eighty-eight countries. One result of this is that viewers are able to observe not only different world views through the portraiture shown, but

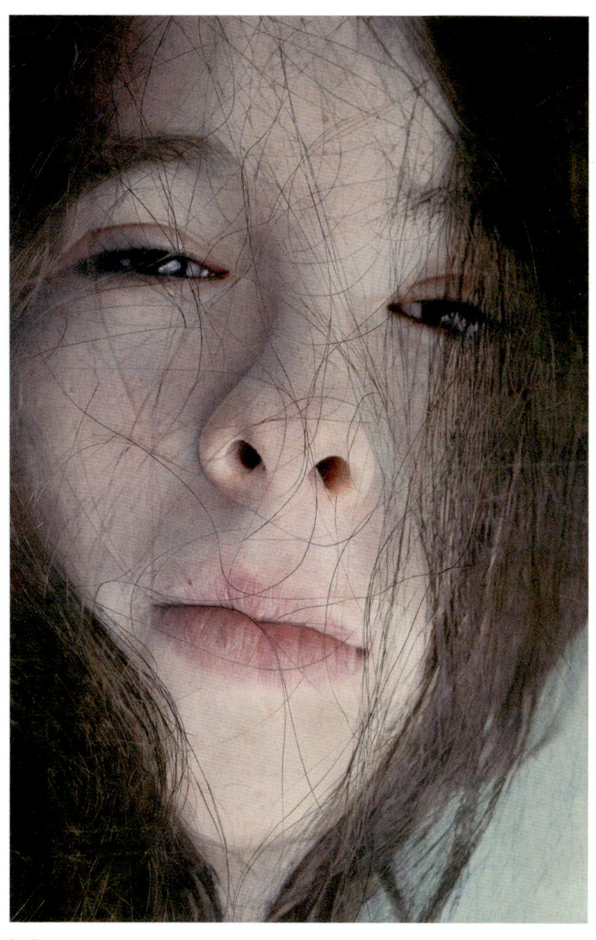

Bertha
by Jesús María Sáez de Vicuña Ochoa, 2017
Oil on canvas, 1500 × 1000mm

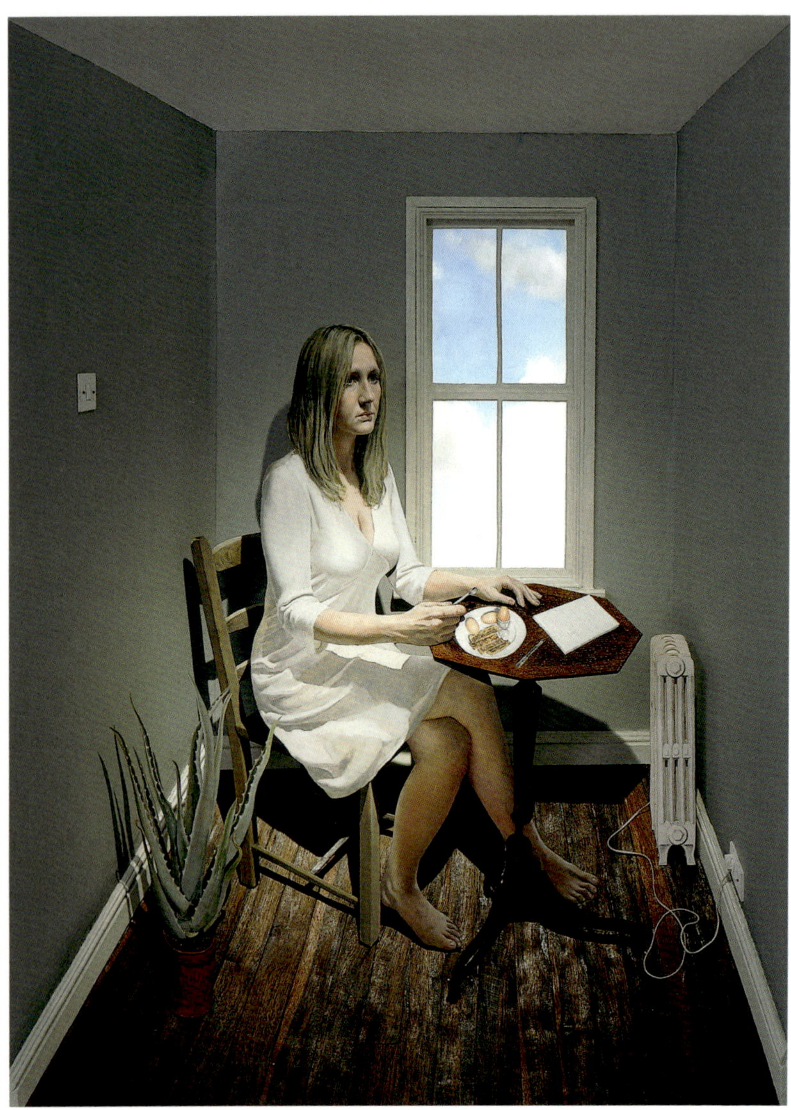

J.K. Rowling
by Stuart Pearson Wright, 2005 (NPG 6723)
Oil on board construction with coloured pencil
on paper, 972 × 720mm

also the different ways in which painting is taught in, say, art schools in Beijing, Florence or Aberdeen. The Travel Award has also undoubtedly enriched further the global dimension of the exhibition and demonstrated how portraiture can provide insight into entire communities as well as the lives of individuals far from our everyday experience; recent examples have included wonderful projects undertaken in Peru, the Netherlands, the United States and Burkina Faso.

During the years in which the BP Portrait Award has evolved this flowering of portrait painting around the world has perhaps appeared to be at risk. In part this is because of a decline in some areas of the teaching of traditional life drawing skills – once considered the bedrock of all great figurative art. It is also the case, however, that over the same period the internet has come to underpin everyone's lives. In this digital age, how we create, consume and share all imagery – but most especially portraits – has changed at a more accelerated rate than at any time in history.

It might have been imagined that with a limitless capacity for manipulating and transmitting digital images of each other, old forms of portrait-making like painting would have become a niche interest or endangered. Happily, quite the opposite appears to be the case and the BP Portrait Award exhibition is a vibrant and positive expression of this (similarly, doom-mongers predicted the death of the book and cinema over the same period but publishing and cinema-going are enjoying something of a renaissance). Part of the reason for this may lie in the appeal of slowing down, as painted portraits require thought, time and personal interaction. The appreciation of them can grow gradually as we look, consider, discuss and return to favourites. They are a supremely social art form and it is perhaps rather ironic that the term 'social media' has come to mean something quite different. However, such media does of course play a key role in sharing enthusiasm for the competition and bringing it to many who cannot actually visit the exhibition.

The BP Portrait Award has also undoubtedly had a direct and positive effect on expanding the National Portrait Gallery collections it is displayed alongside, as winning artists and a number of those included in the exhibition subsequently receive commissions. There are many excellent examples that have emerged over the years and only a couple can be mentioned here. One of the most intriguing is undoubtedly Stuart

Pearson Wright's portrait of J.K. Rowling, which was painted in 2005. Pearson Wright won the BP Portrait Award in 2001 and the commission to paint the phenomenally successful author of the *Harry Potter* series followed on from this. He visited her in Edinburgh and created a spatially complex and rather surreal work, which places the writer in a claustrophobic room, while the cloudscape beyond the window perhaps suggests a limitless world of imaginative possibilities. More directly confrontational and successful in a very different way was the 2006 portrait of Johnson Gideon Beharry by Emma Wesley, whose work was selected for the BP Portrait Award exhibition the previous year. Lance Corporal Beharry was awarded the Victoria Cross for outstanding gallantry displayed in Iraq in 2005. The resulting portrait is a powerful painting of great dignity and sensitivity.

Through inclusion in the exhibition and receiving such commissions, painters achieve another form of recognition distinct from that discussed above, which focuses on the sitters: an enhancement of their professional standing and the opportunities that are then open to them. I have been lucky enough to discuss with a number of artists how this has led to new commissions, often far beyond the arena of portrait galleries. At a time when it is so difficult to establish a sustainable creative career, the effect has been genuinely transformative.

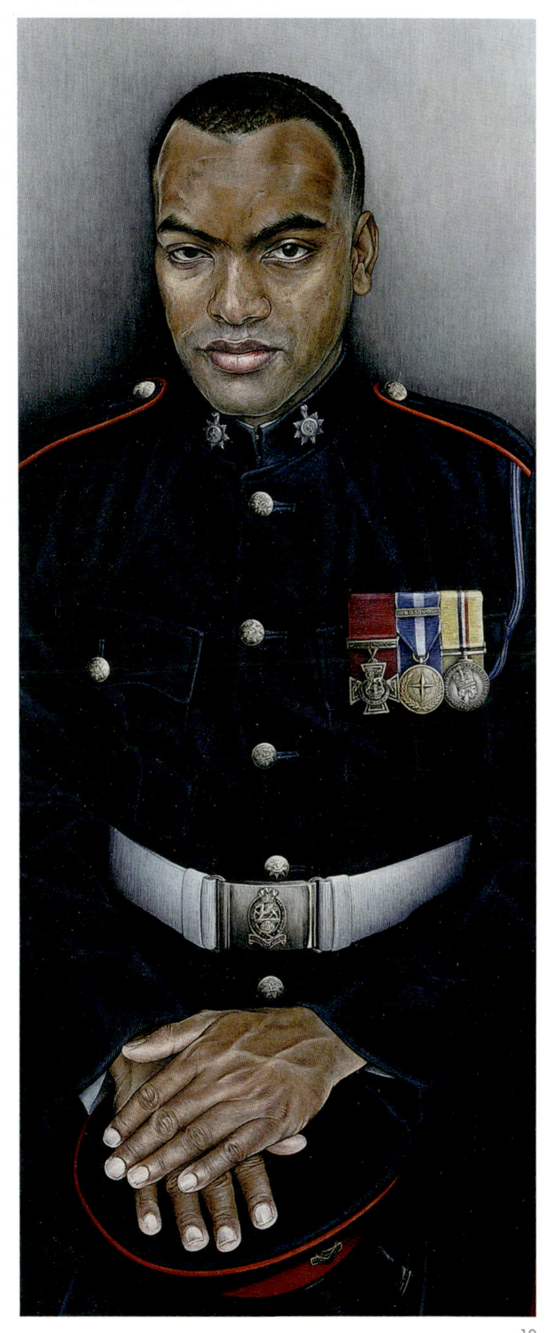

Johnson Gideon Beharry
by Emma Wesley, 2006 (NPG 6803)
Acrylic on panel, 804 × 336mm

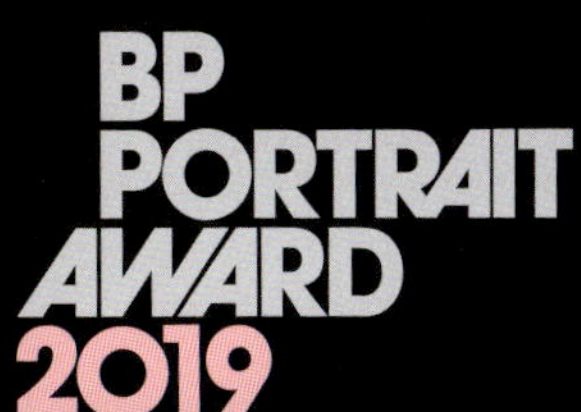

BP PORTRAIT AWARD 2019

The Portrait Award, in its fortieth year at the National Portrait Gallery and its thirtieth year of sponsorship by BP, is an annual event aimed at encouraging artists to focus on and develop the theme of portraiture in their work. The competition is open to everyone aged eighteen and over, in recognition of the outstanding and innovative work currently being produced by artists of all ages.

THE JUDGES

Chair: Nicholas Cullinan,
Director, National Portrait Gallery

Gaylene Gould
Head of Cinemas and Events,
BFI Southbank

Gary Hume
Artist

Alison Smith
Chief Curator, National Portrait Gallery

Des Violaris,
Director, UK Arts & Culture, BP

Zoé Whitley
Senior Curator, Hayward Gallery,
Southbank Centre

THE PRIZES
The BP Portrait Awards are:

First Prize
£35,000, plus at the Gallery's discretion a commission worth £7,000.
Charlie Schaffer

Second Prize
£12,000
Carl-Martin Sandvold

Third Prize
£10,000
Massimiliano Pironti

BP Young Artist Award
£9,000
Emma Hopkins

PRIZEWINNING PORTRAITS

Imara in Her Winter Coat
Charlie Schaffer

Oil on canvas
1200 × 900mm

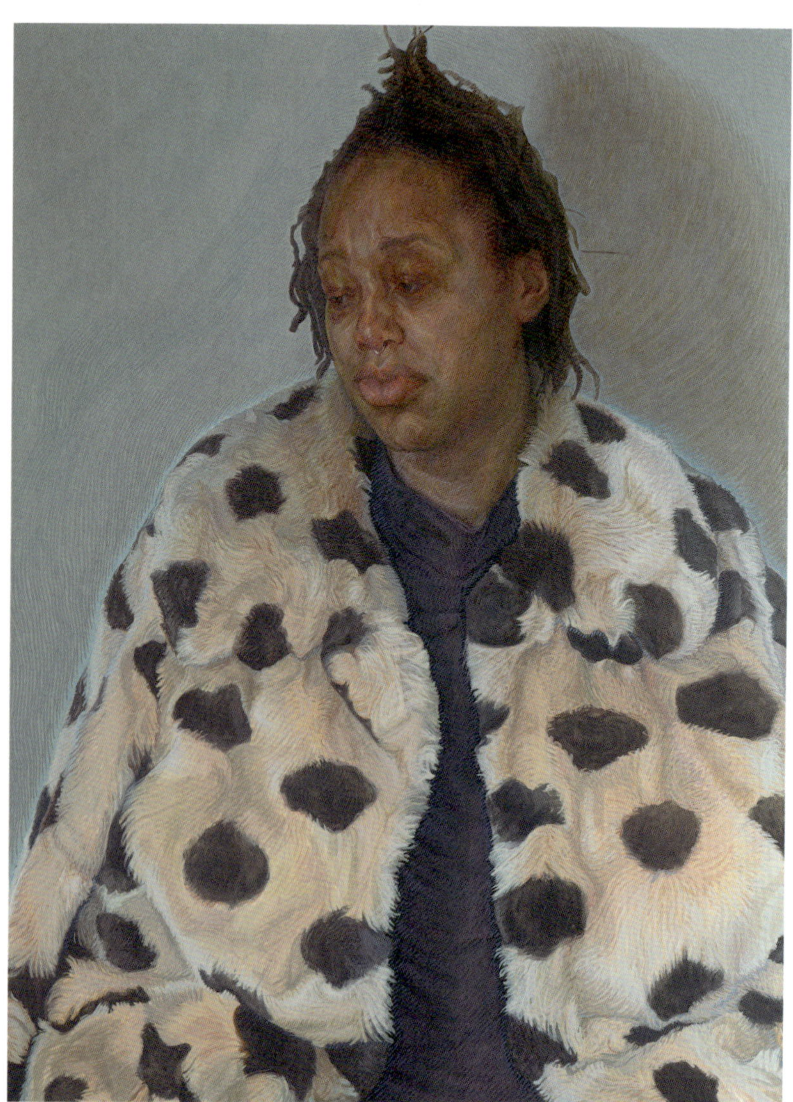

Charlie Schaffer considers his painting to be a 'kind of therapy' in which the portrait is entirely a reflection of the relationship between artist and sitter. The act of painting someone allows a 'very intense and specific' attachment to be formed, outweighing the significance of the actual physical portrait, which is 'more of a record, or by-product' of that connection.

'I don't aim to capture the essence of the sitter, nor create a likeness. It's about recording the experience of our relationship,' explains Schaffer. 'A human is not an inanimate object; people are interesting because they're people, not because of how they look. During each sitting, there is constant conversation. I'm led by how much we share. Without talk, it's like a still life.'

Originally from London, Schaffer studied at Central Saint Martins before graduating with a degree in Fine Art from the University of Brighton in 2014. He has gone on to win the Brian Botting Prize 'for an outstanding representation of the human figure' an unprecedented three times.

In choosing a sitter, Schaffer selects only those he finds to be emotionally or intellectually stimulating and who are willing to talk about life's biggest issues. His winning entry portrays Imara, an English Literature student he met after moving permanently to Brighton. 'She immediately struck me as someone who is uncompromisingly open and who wants to learn about anything and everything.'

The sittings took place over four months, with Imara posing in her warmest winter coat to withstand the studio's cold conditions. Schaffer set out to paint only her face, but subsequently added the coat after being inspired by Titian's *Portrait of Girolamo Fracastoro* in the National Gallery, London, with its pyramidal composition and the subject's similar attire.

'It was an emotionally fraught period for both of us,' he recalls. 'I was in a deep depression for the duration of the painting and Imara was going through a lot of emotional turmoil too. This painting gave us structure and friendship when we needed it the most.'

The portrait marked a new way of applying paint for Schaffer, who mixed oils with a medium for the first time. 'Previously I feared that painting with a medium would create too long a pause between seeing, mixing a colour and applying the paint. However, using pure paint caused the paintings to become very thick and so the drawing was lost in the texture,' he explains. 'Here, I could retain every line made, forcing me to look even closer and have a real connection with every mark made rather than relying on texture to give substance.'

The pair struck up a close friendship and Imara is now sitting for a second portrait, in keeping with the artist's belief that the personal relationship is paramount. 'When each painting is finished, it suddenly becomes only what it can ever be – just a picture. I no longer have an emotional connection to it,' he says. 'This is why, on the same day as showing the final painting to a sitter, we will immediately begin the next.'

Interview by Richard McClure

The Crown
Carl-Martin Sandvold

Oil on linen
500 × 400mm

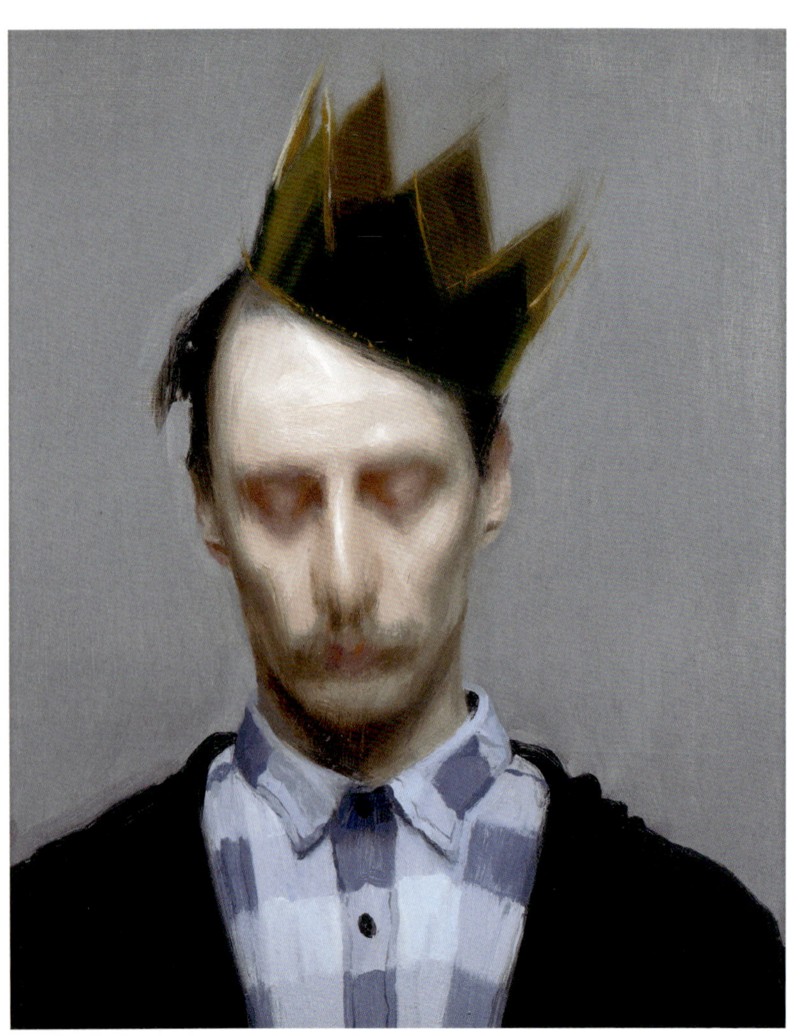

Carl-Martin Sandvold's first artistic efforts took place on the streets of Oslo, where he made urban street art during his teenage years. 'I spent around five or six years being very into graffiti,' he recalls. 'It meant everything to me at the time, so when I quit in my twenties it felt absolutely necessary to substitute it with a different kind of painting.'

Sandvold found that substitute in portrait-making, drawn to the practice because of its 'potential emotional impact'. Beginning his training in Norway, he continued his studies at the Florence Academy of Art and the Grand Central Academy of Art in New York, before returning to Florence for a stint at the Charles H. Cecil Studios.

'I don't believe that art needs to be purely figurative, but I generally respond more to work that at least has some strong figurative elements,' he says. 'The expression of emotion is crucial to me and that communication is far easier through recognisable symbols.'

His entry is a self-portrait in oils and reflects his interest in 'the challenges of life, the strangeness of being alive and other existential issues'. Central to his portraiture is the belief that we are all trying to reconcile the love of life with the knowledge of death. 'The crown symbolises the peak of power, achievement and material abundance. In this portrait, it suggests that none of these things really solve anything.'

The painting was finished in four days, in contrast to previous works that have taken him months or years. 'I recently came out of a long stretch of disappointment, feeling that I was putting so much into my work but it was not paying off,' he says. 'I stood there with a bunch of large, tedious-looking canvases on which I'd laboured day after day, not feeling they had … the power I was looking for.'

In response, he resolved to complete as many paintings as possible in a year. 'I needed a way of working that would make the pictures bold, fresh and full of life. Now I am painting many relatively fast versions of the same image. It is new to me, but it feels exciting. The fact that this portrait was done over a short period of time helped me to maintain a certain amount of life in the picture. The composition is simple and strong and I think it reads powerfully from a distance.'

Sandvold's studio is located on the site of Edvard Munch's former estate on the outskirts of Oslo, which the Norwegian government has turned into a subsidised housing and studio complex for artists.

'Working in my studio can be quite intense at times,' he says. 'Painting is the most wonderful thing, and it is important to maintain the belief in what you are trying to do. You need to sustain focus and stamina. It's important to pursue something for the right reasons, not because it is in fashion or you think it will be met with praise.'

Interview by Richard McClure

Quo vadis?
Massimiliano Pironti

Oil on aluminium
900 × 600mm

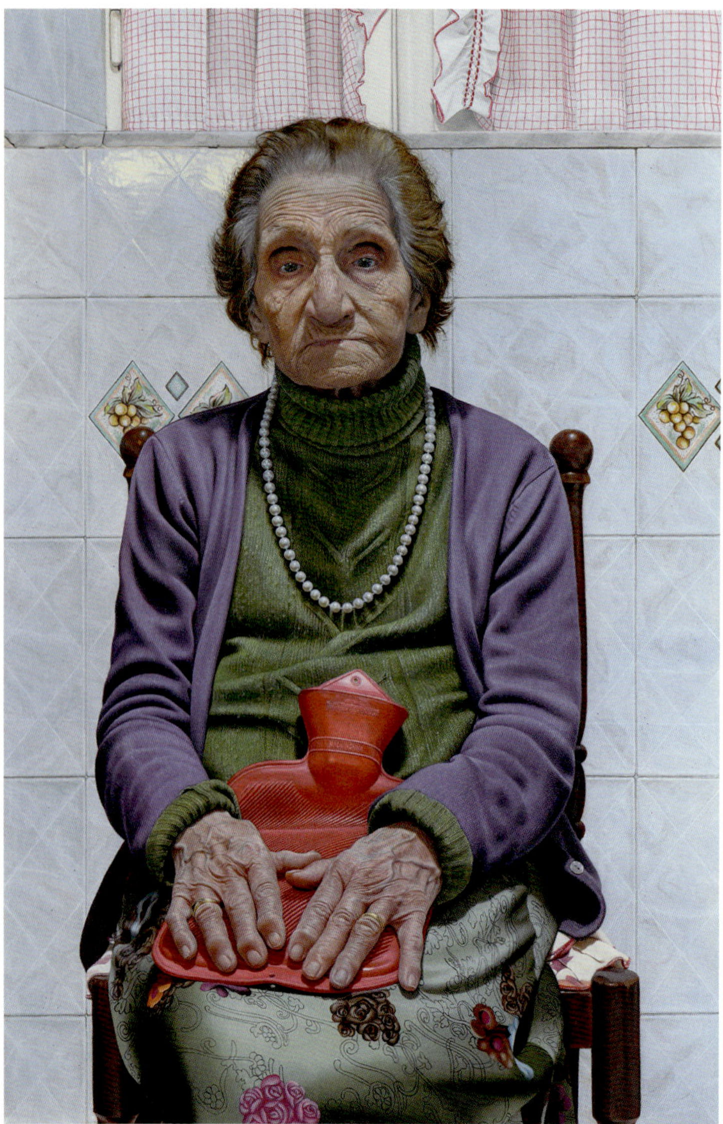

Born in Colleferro, an industrial town south of Rome, Massimiliano Pironti was inspired to become an artist by his early exposure to famous artworks during frequent daytrips to the city. 'I would go to Rome and be enchanted by its beauty,' he recalls. 'As a child I'd walk around and draw the most beautiful statues, or enter a church to find incredible works by Caravaggio or Michelangelo.'

Pironti taught himself oil painting as a teenager before attending an art school in Frosinone, where he focused his attention on portraiture. 'My objective was to be like the Old Masters; they were my idols, the example of perfection,' he says. 'I wanted to give a soul to my paintings, but at the same time tell stories of people.'

Painting is not his sole occupation. At the age of sixteen, he began to dance professionally and he is now well-known in Italy for his performances in musical theatre, including *Cats* and *Saturday Night Fever*. He currently lives in Germany where he has been appearing in a long-running production of the Disney musical *Tarzan*.

'My different worlds are very important to me. With painting, I can meditate. With dance and singing, I can throw out the emotions. It has been hard to balance the two, but they are both fundamental parts of my life.'

In 2018, he exhibited a painting of a fellow dancer in the BP Portrait Award. In this year's competition, his entry depicts his maternal grandmother, Vincenza, a former miller and factory worker now aged ninety-five. Pironti made sketches and took photographs in the kitchen of her home in the town of Gavignano, returning to his studio in Germany for the painting process.

'My grandmother is an example of strength, dignity and authority. Every wrinkle tells her story and I wanted to capture her image to freeze time. This portrait is truly important to me. It touches emotional chords.'

The portrait is painted in oils on an aluminium panel, a smooth surface that Pironti prefers for his technique of using very thin layers of colour and overlapping glazes. 'Painting on aluminium is not easy at all, the colour slips a lot, but the end result is fantastic. I am obsessed by the details and getting as close as possible to reality. I want to create the illusion that the painting can at some point take life.'

As with all his portraits, Pironti set out to lower the viewer's eye towards the centre of the picture, depicting the figure as though seen from below. 'I like to confer majesty on the sitter, as though they were on a throne. The influence of Rome's sacred images must still be imprinted on my mind.'

He also notes the portrait's symbolism: the spiritual connotations of the open window and the vanitas-like hot water bottle representing passing time. 'The water that now warms my grandmother's hands sooner or later will cool,' he says. 'Like life, it comes and goes.'

Interview by Richard McClure

Sophie and Carla
Emma Hopkins

Oil on polyester
1520 × 920mm

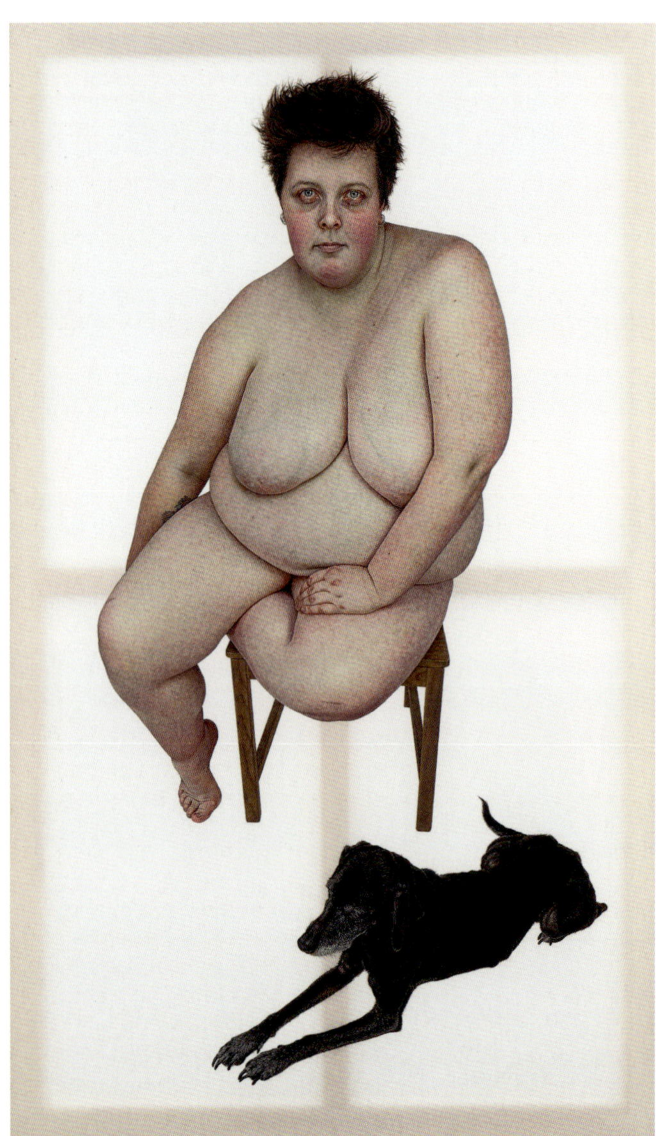

Emma Hopkins turned to portrait-painting after graduating with a degree in Make-up and Prosthetics for Performance from the University of the Arts, London. Her expertise has fed directly into her painting, which focuses almost exclusively on nude portraits and studies of human flesh.

Hopkins was born in Brighton in 1989 and is fascinated by themes of anatomy, psychology and mortality. Listing Egon Schiele, Frida Kahlo and Paul McCarthy as influences, she endeavours to 'paint people from the inside out' in a bid to uncover the relationships we have with our body, mind and emotions.

'I want to understand as much as I can about what it means to be human,' she says. 'We are not just the clothed person we present to the world. We are the mind and body that we inhabit. There are aspects that connect us all and we are also unique individuals. I moved into painting portraits because it is a celebration of this.'

Hopkins is self-taught and first exhibited in a staff show at the Chelsea Arts Club while working behind the bar. She is a member of the Royal Society of Portrait Painters and is now the recipient of the BP Young Artist Award for her study of photographer Sophie Mayanne with her dog Carla.

The sitter is known for Behind the Scars, a photography project about people's scars and the stories behind them. It's an interest that Hopkins shares, and the pair became friends as a result of this mutual thread. 'When I paint people, it is important for me to feel free to make pieces of artwork and not objects of flattery. Sophie wasn't afraid of other people seeing her body. If a person can ignite my emotions and my curiosity, then I'm drawn in.'

When working, Hopkins uses a variety of materials to make multiple interpretations of her sitters and thus free herself from the constraints of 'one way of painting or one idea'. Noticing how Sophie would perch on a chair, she asked her to adopt the same pose for the portrait, which was painted in oil on a translucent fabric.

'Sophie often sits on one leg while the other hangs down and I loved the subtle asymmetry and the descending flow of weight that it gave to the body. Carla's position was very much decided by Carla. Luckily at one point she held a position that knitted in perfectly with the chair and that mirrored the flow of Sophie's body. Something that I really wanted to capture in Sophie's face was strength and vulnerability.'

At a time when images of the 'perfect body' continue to dominate the media, Hopkins hopes her portraits act as an antidote. 'So many of my sitters have begun the process feeling self-conscious; they don't understand why I would want to paint them,' she says. 'But, after time, they see what I see – the beauty in their body and why it should be celebrated. That has really encouraged me to keep going.'

Interview by Richard McClure

SELECTED PORTRAITS

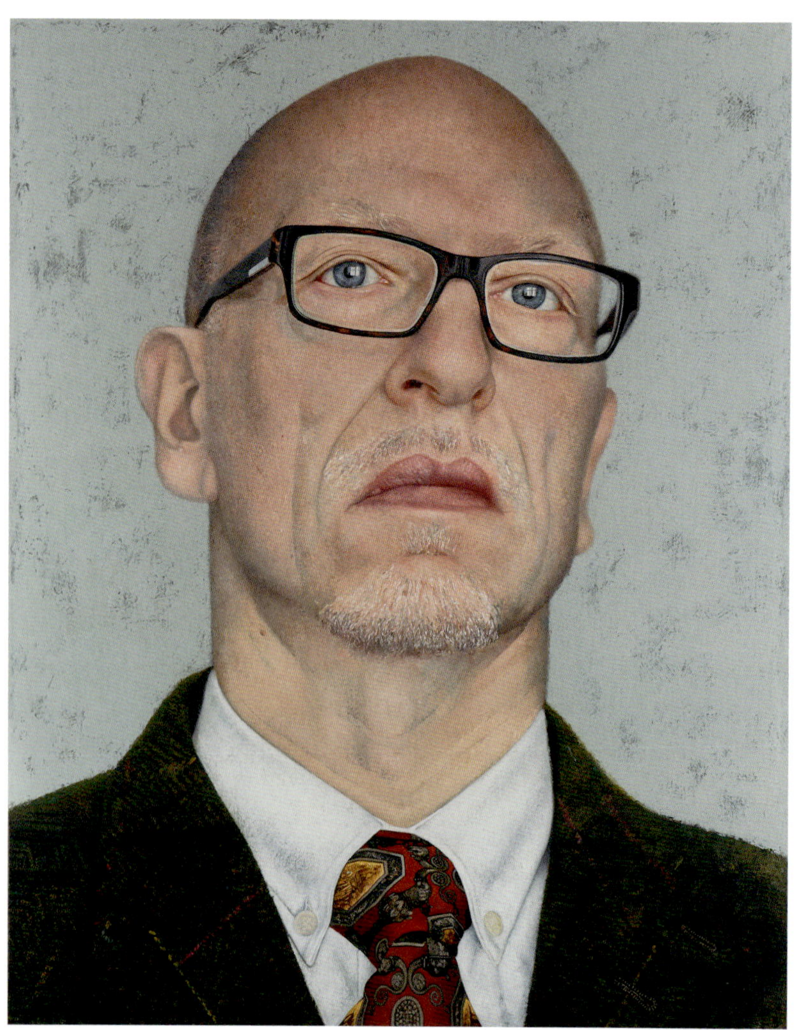

Saskia
Jennifer Anderson
Oil on board
630 × 610mm

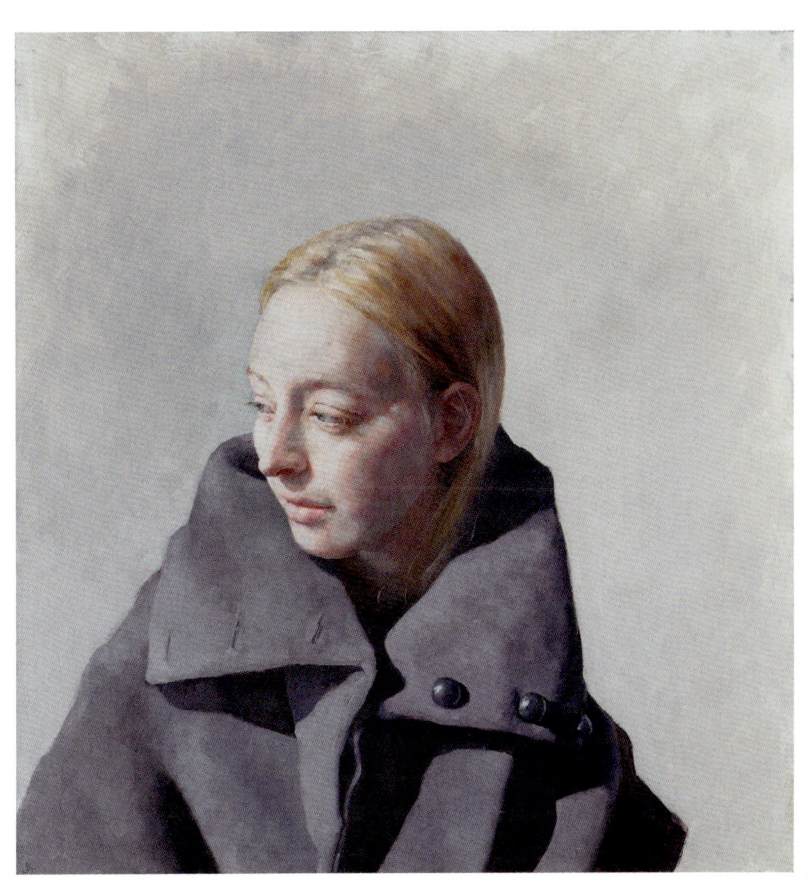

Girl with Headphones
Jane Beharrell

Oil on wood panel
260 × 210mm

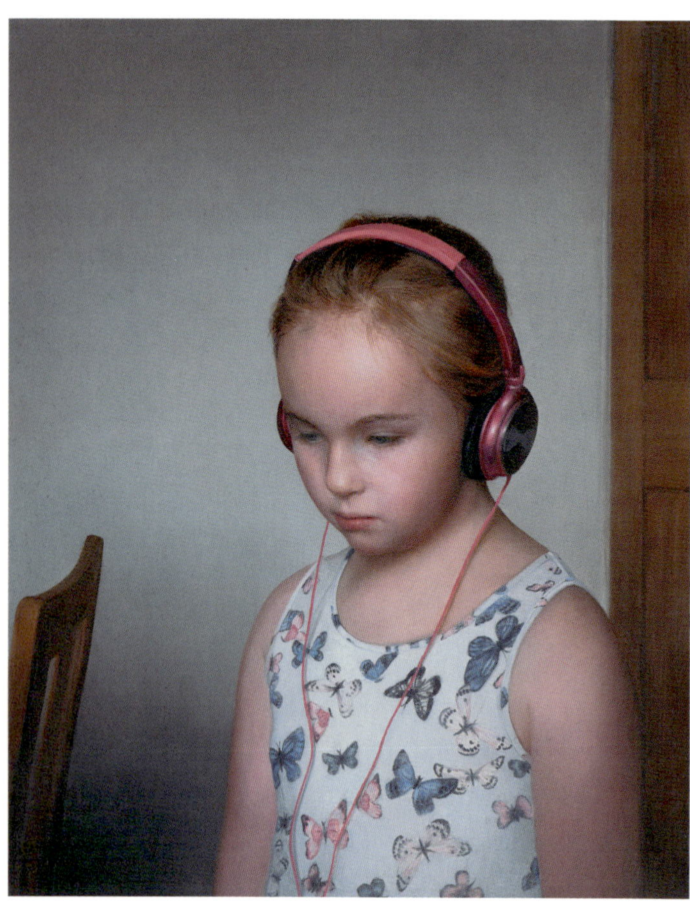

Rumination
Frances Bell

Oil on canvas
920 × 1210mm

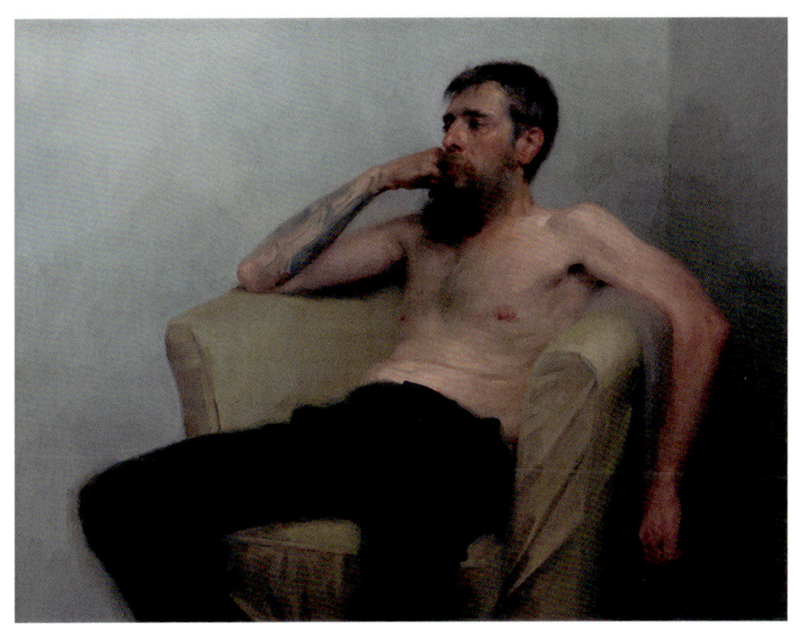

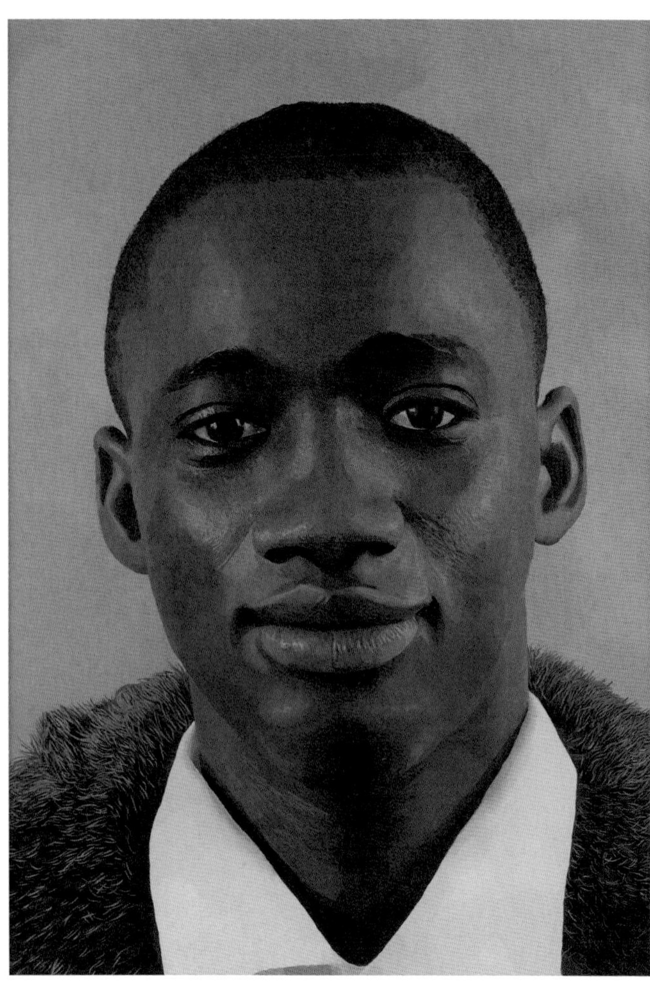

Mixed media (oil, acrylic and spray on board)
800 × 600mm

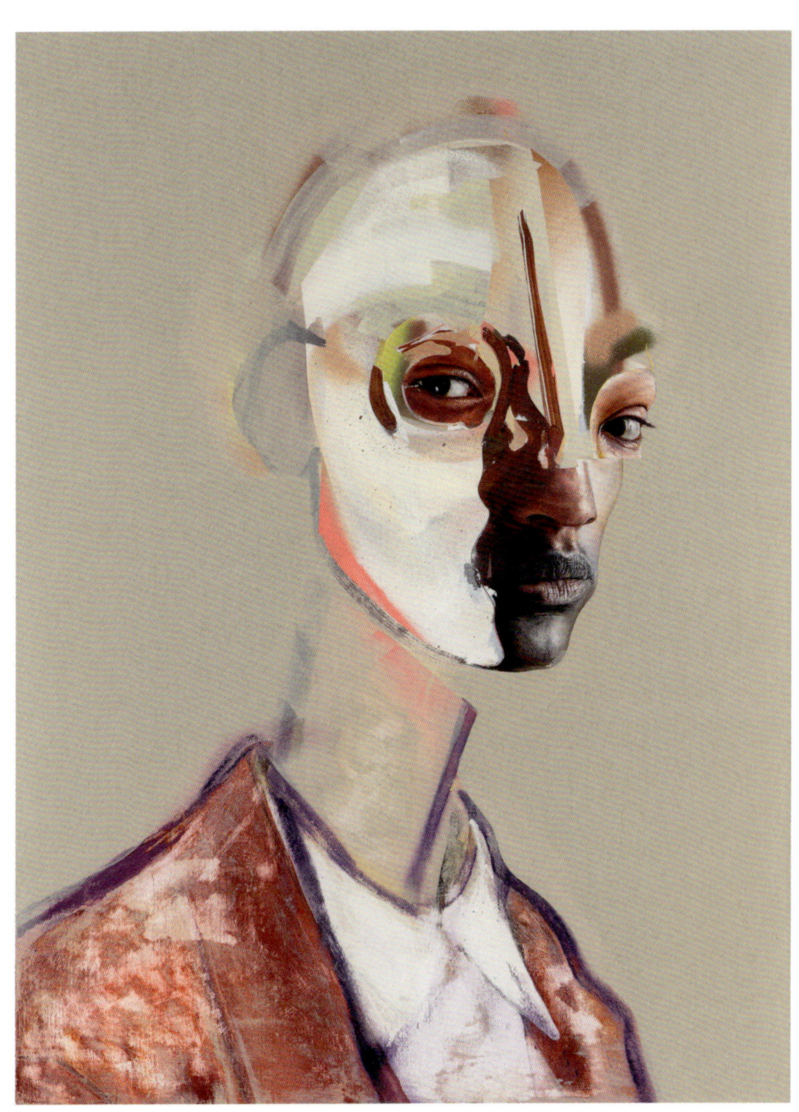

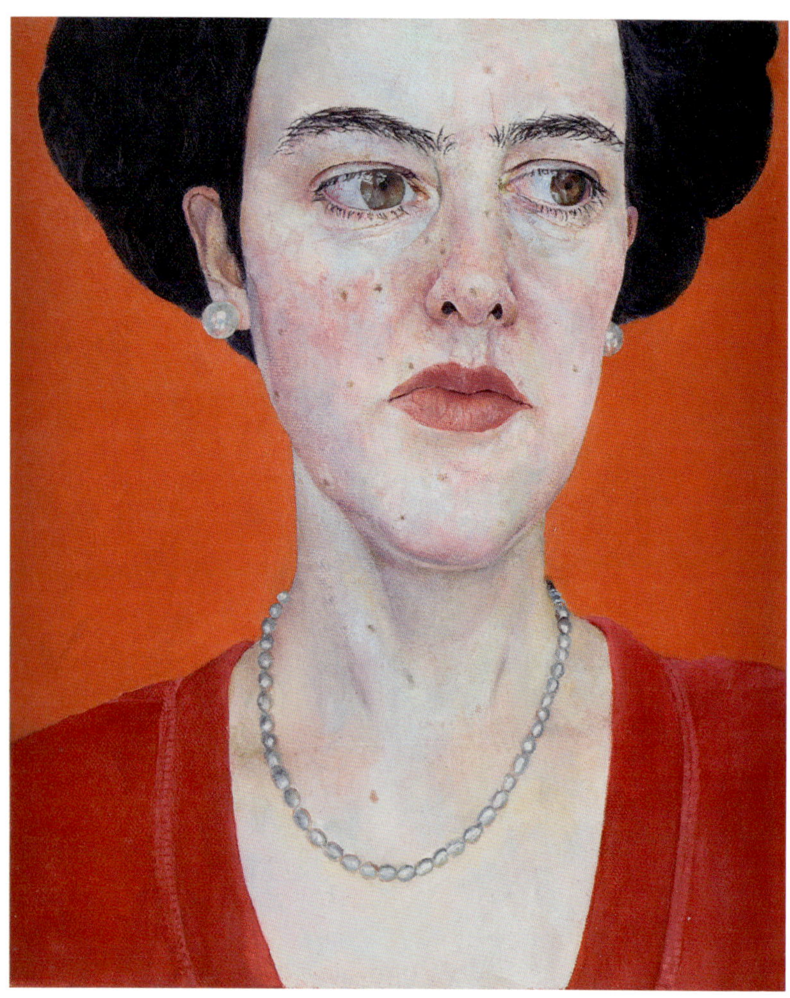

Ian
Simon Thomas Braiden

Oil on panel
250 × 200mm

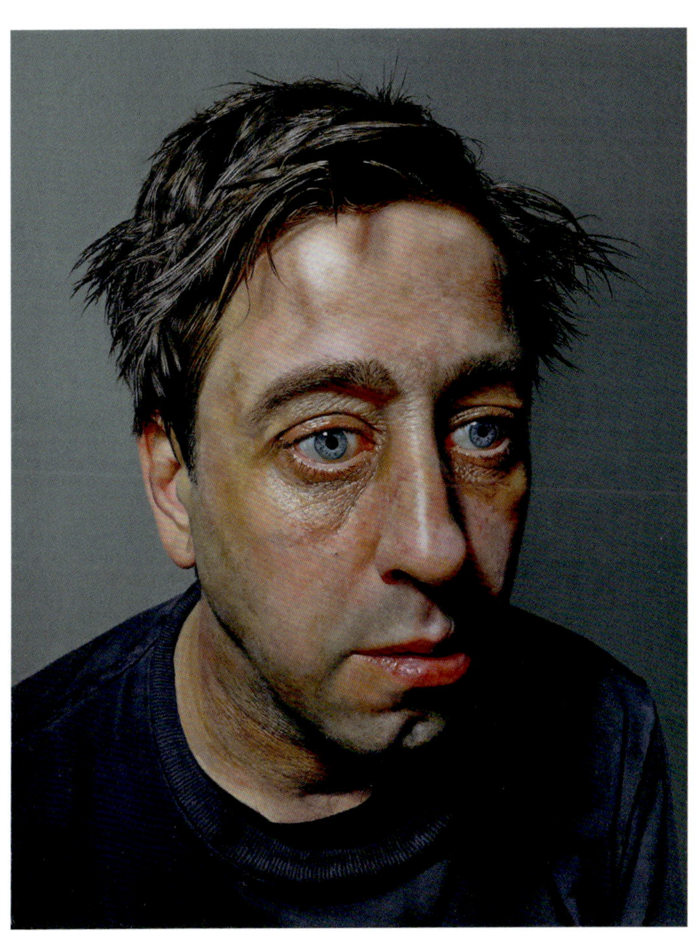

Aurelio
Iván Chacón

Oil on canvas
1060 × 900mm

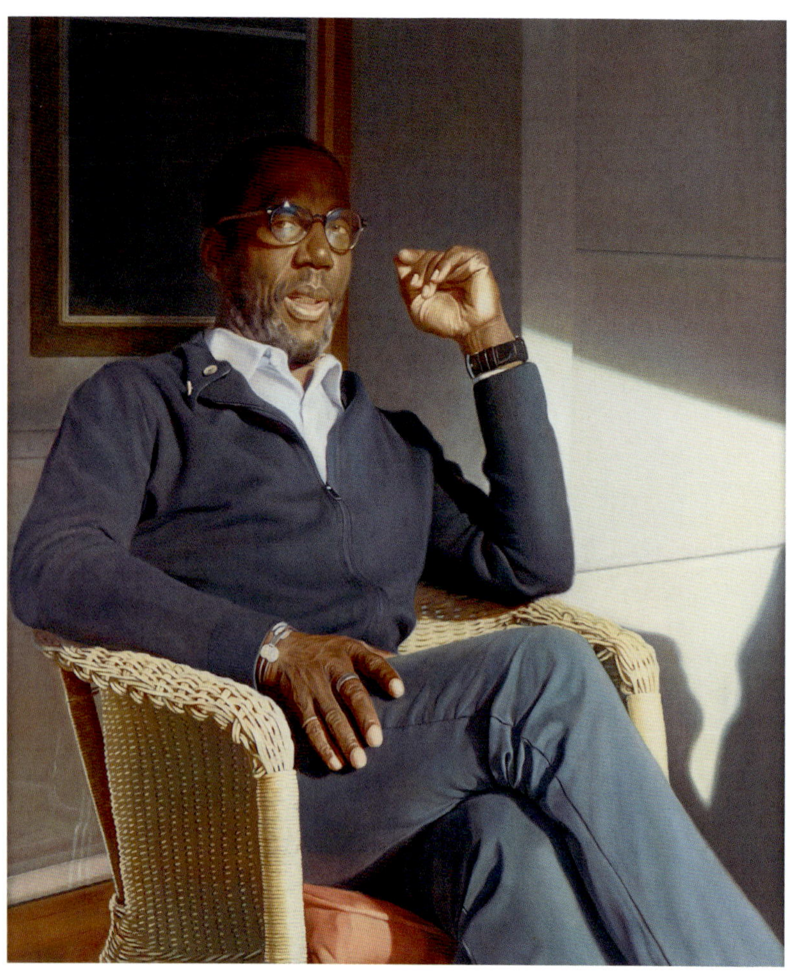

Self-Portrait
Sheng Chieh Chou

Oil on canvas
730 × 910mm

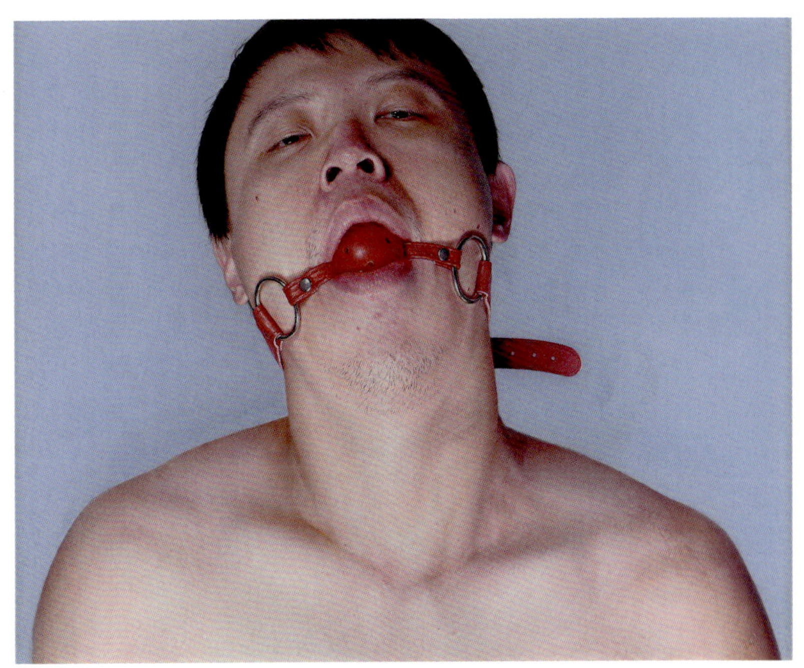

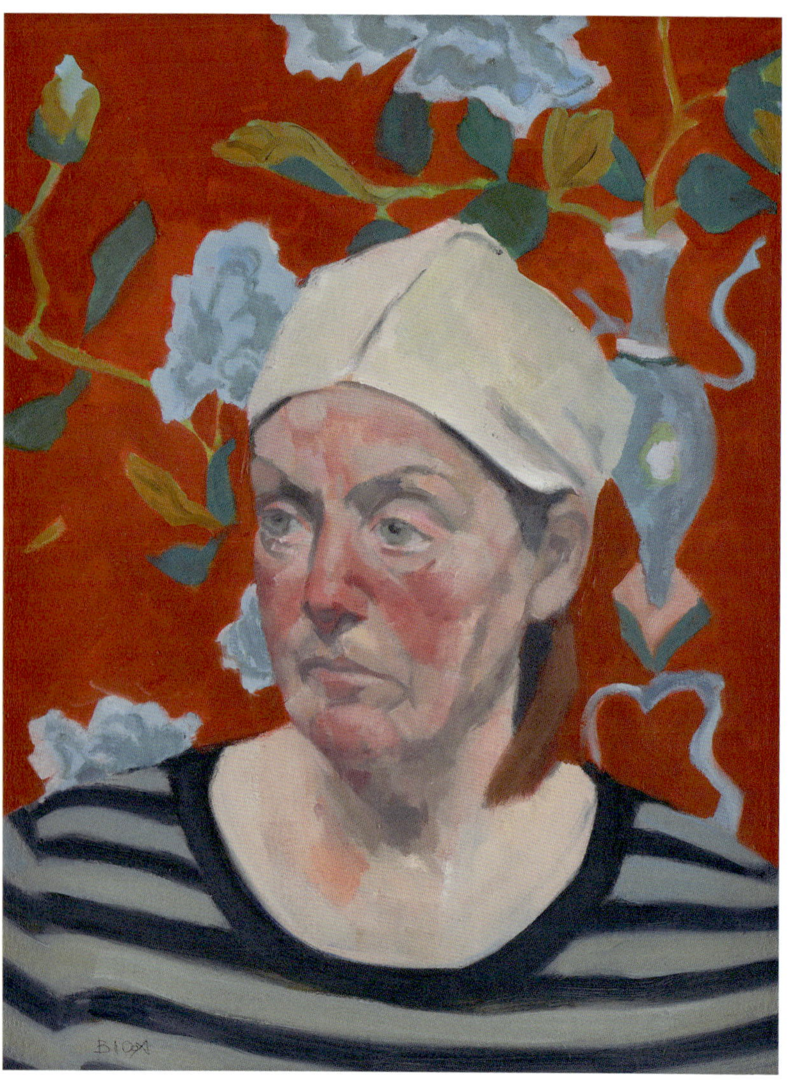

Milo
Denis Dalesio

Acrylic on panel
250 × 200mm

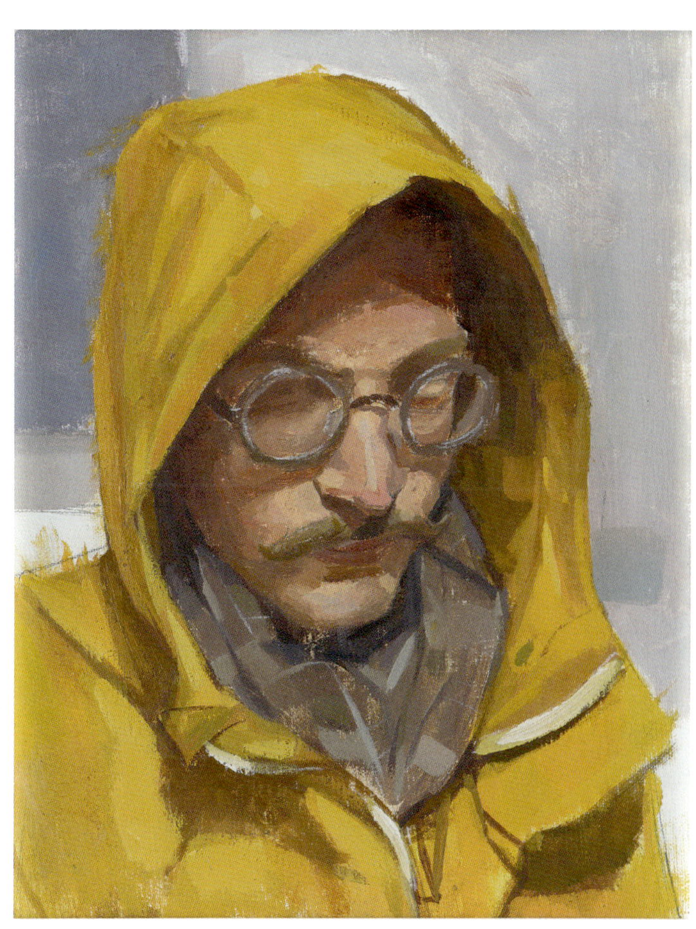

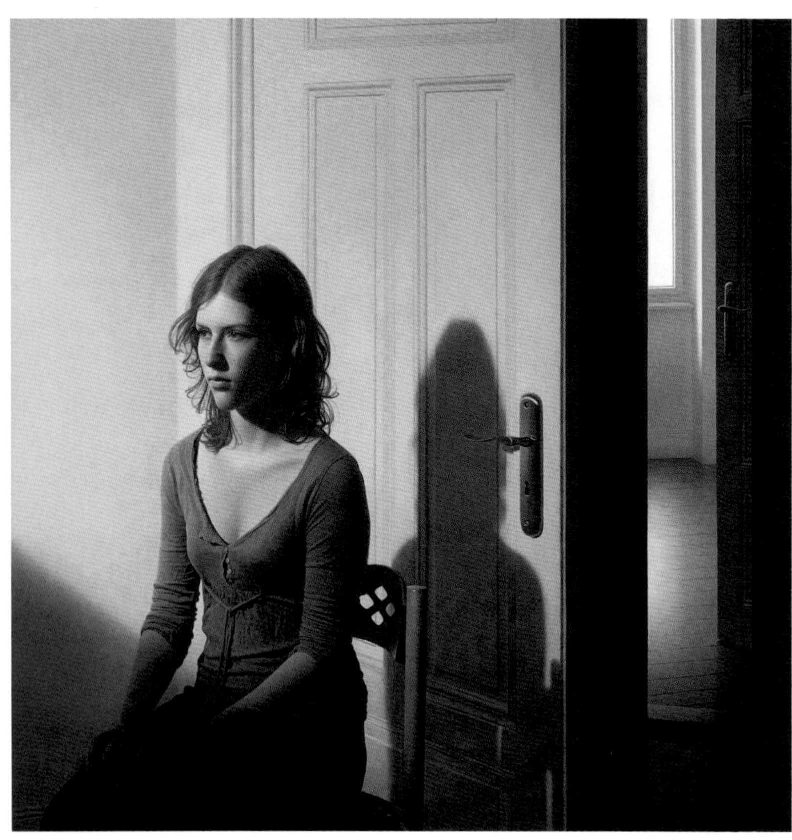

Eden (Protection)
David J. Eichenberg

Oil on aluminium
330 × 250mm

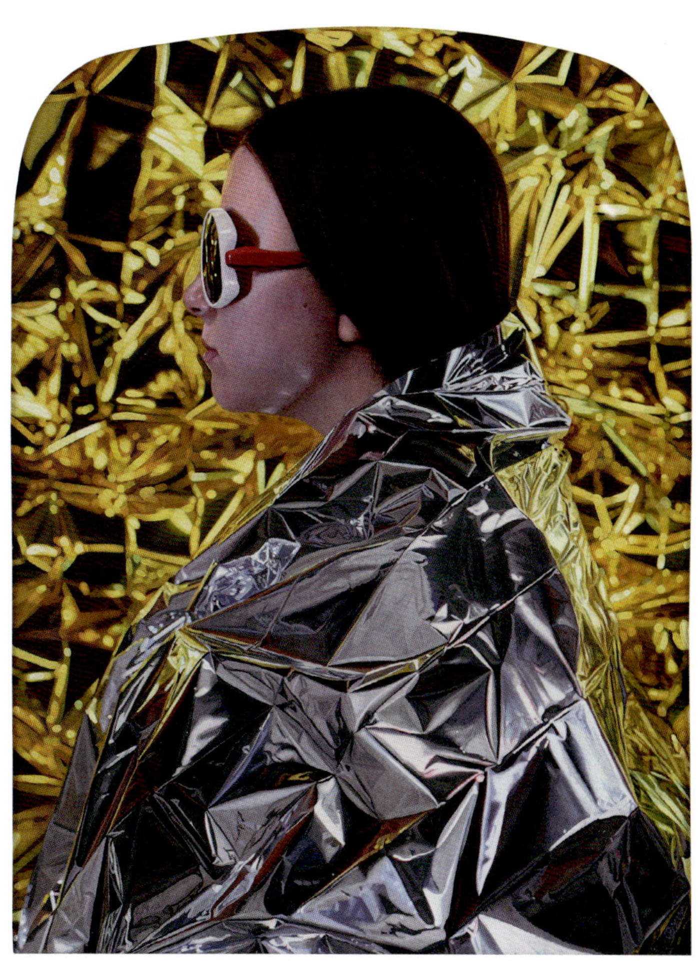

Marcus
Vanessa Garwood

Oil on canvas
1520 × 1220mm

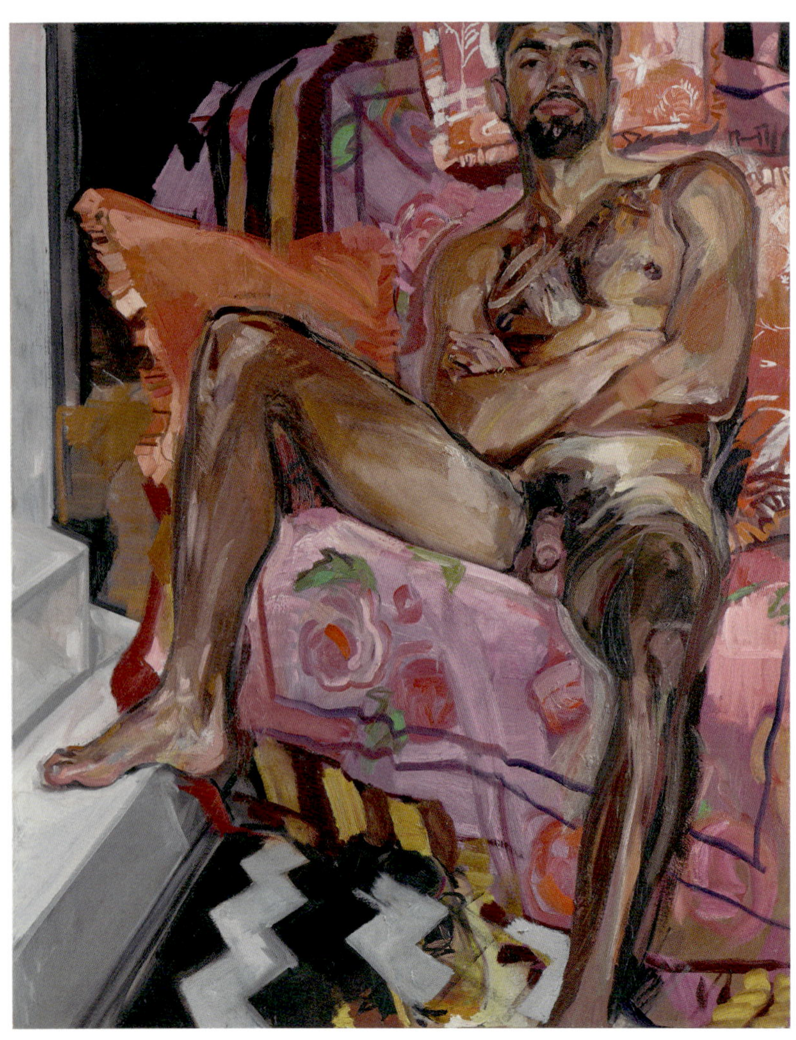

Oil on board
400 × 300mm

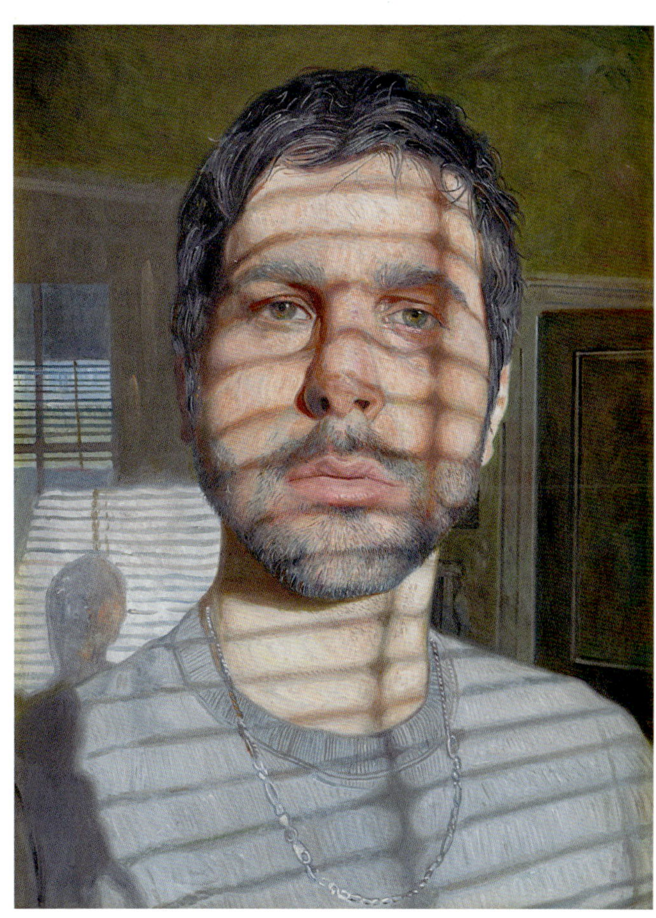

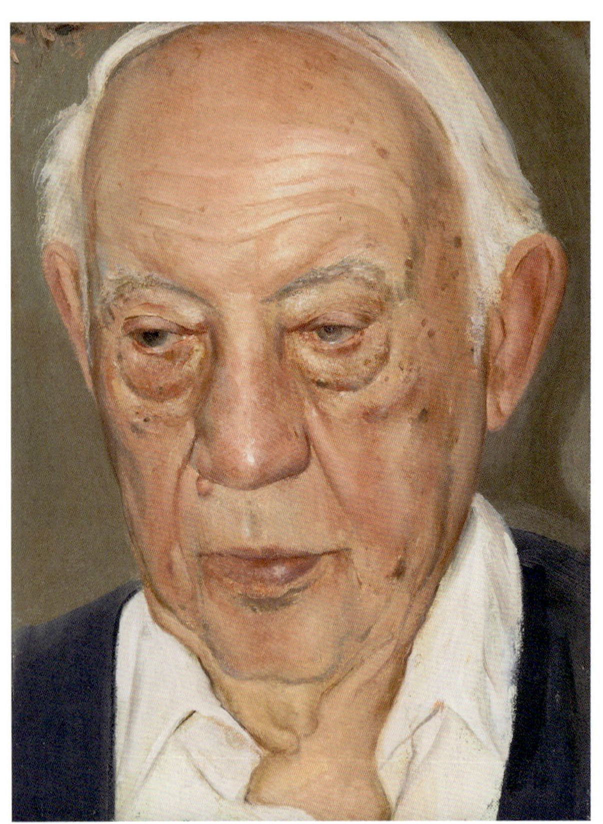

Arcus
Brendan H. Johnston

Oil on linen
610 × 580mm

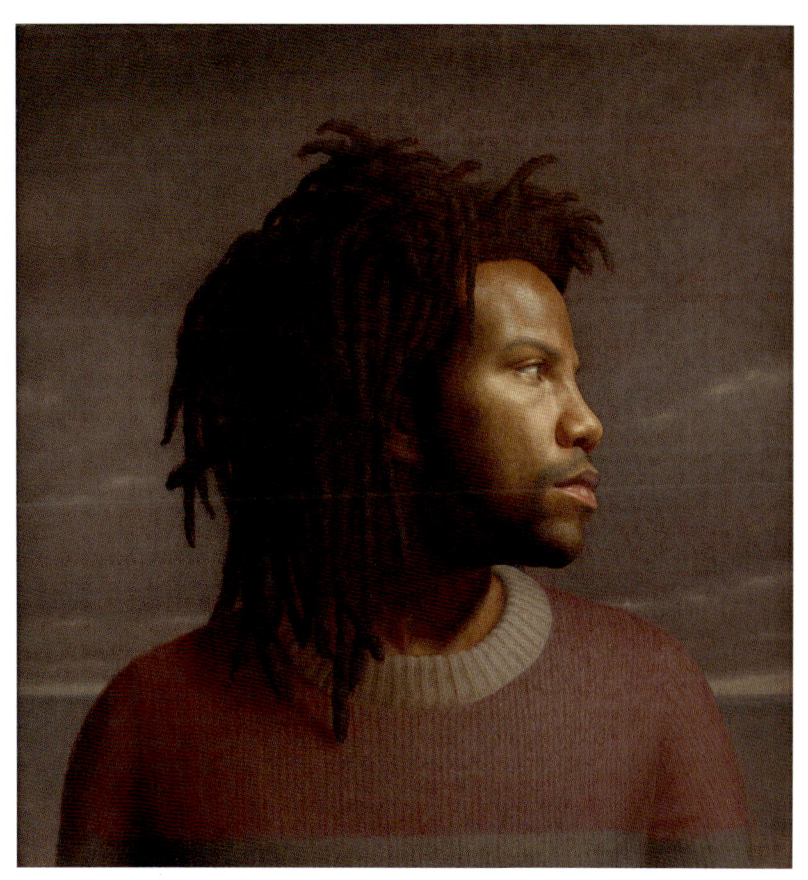

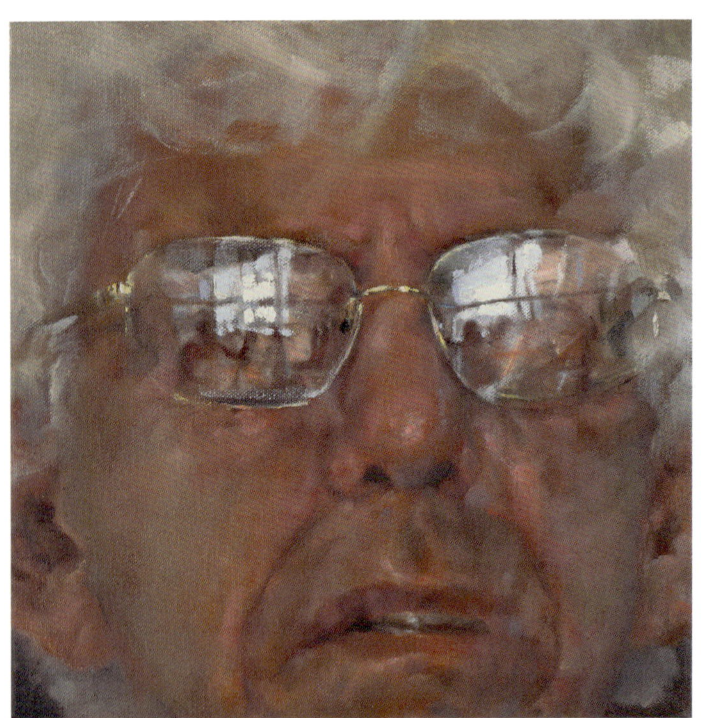

Father with Partner
Marco Krauwinkel

Oil on linen
780 × 1100mm

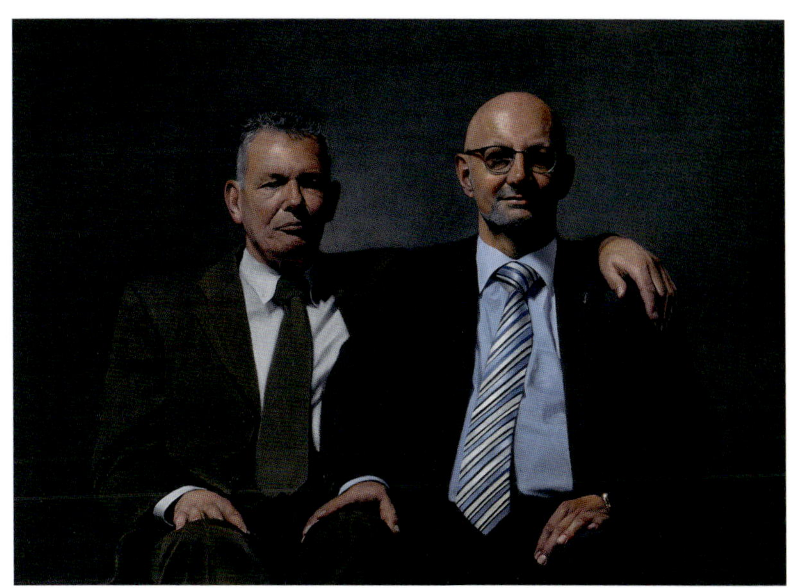

Dieja
Scott Lancashire

Oil on board
410 × 300mm

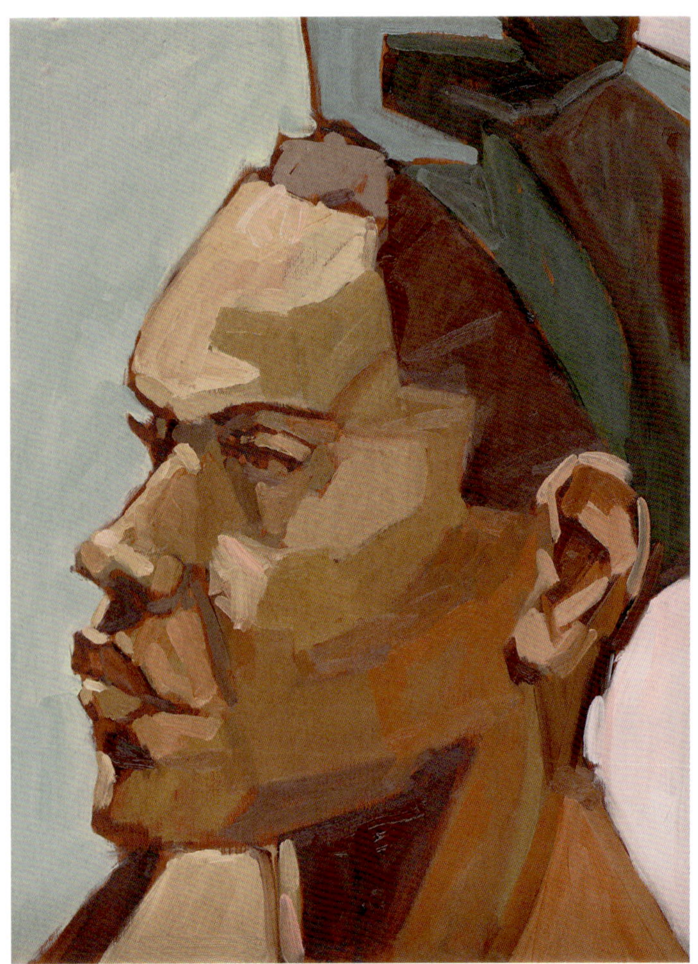

Artist Frank Bowling
Tedi Lena

Oil on canvas
910 × 720mm

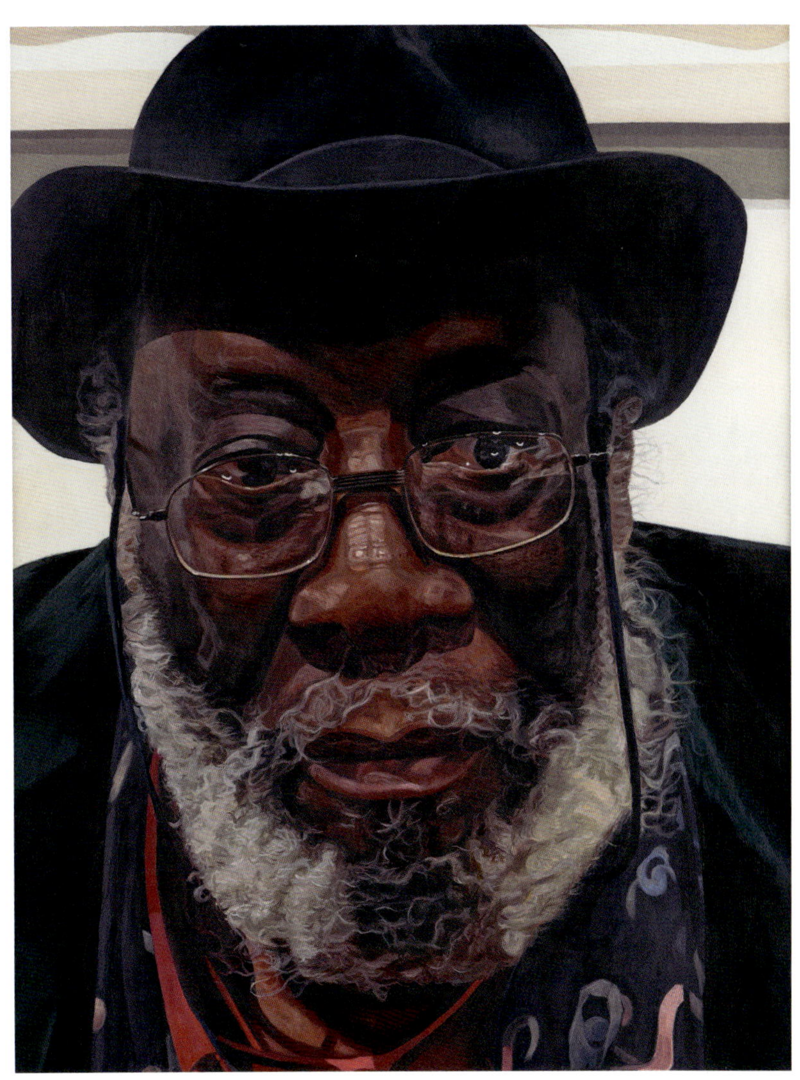

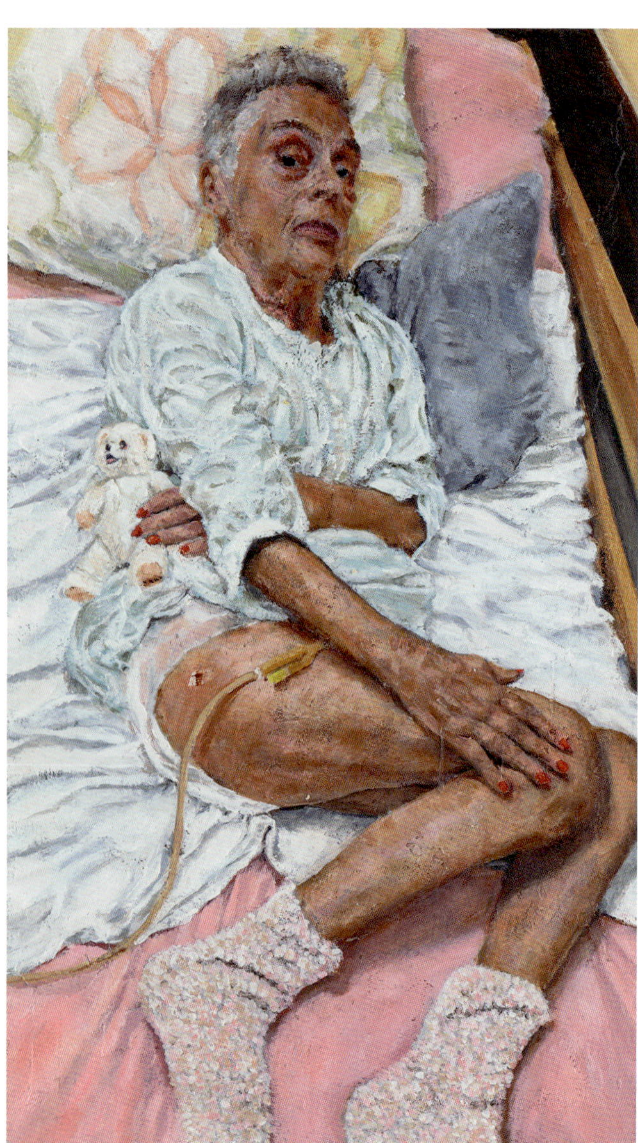

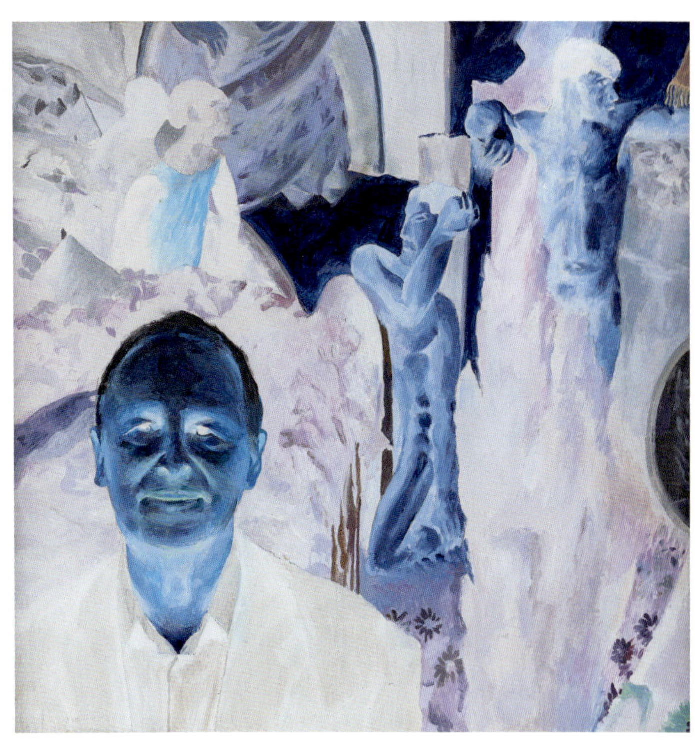

Oil on canvas
1320 × 1020mm

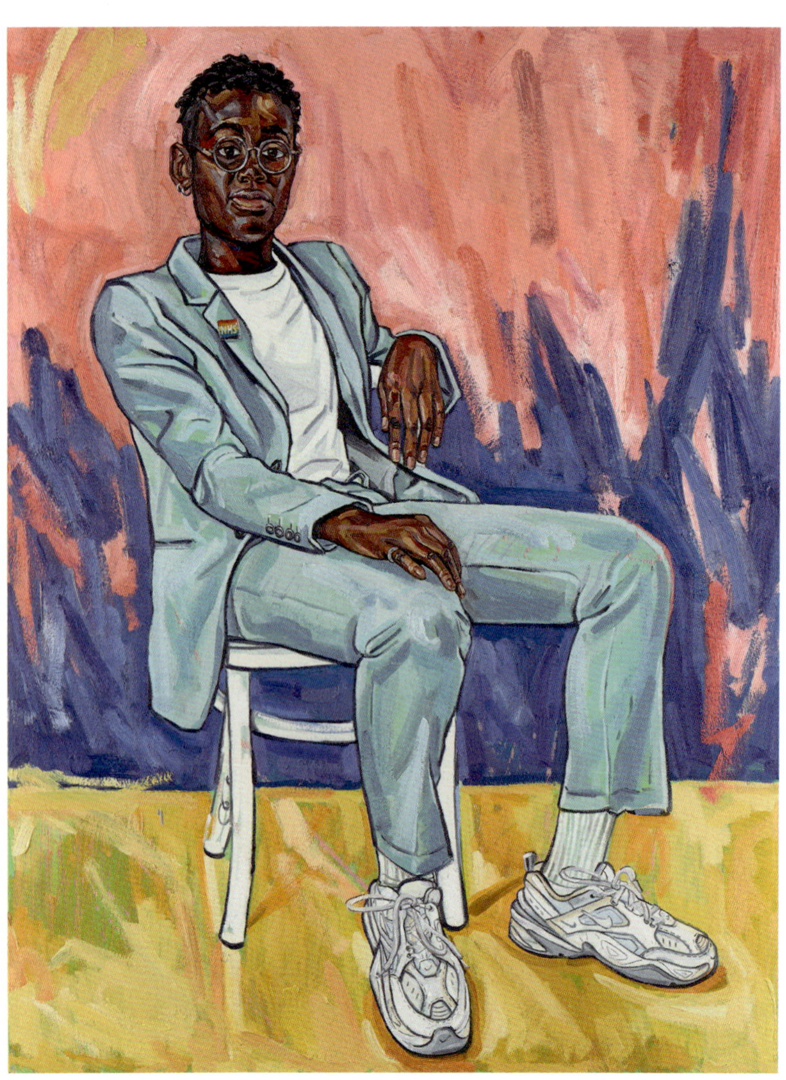

Untitled (November)
Daniel Nelis

Oil on panel
217 × 170mm

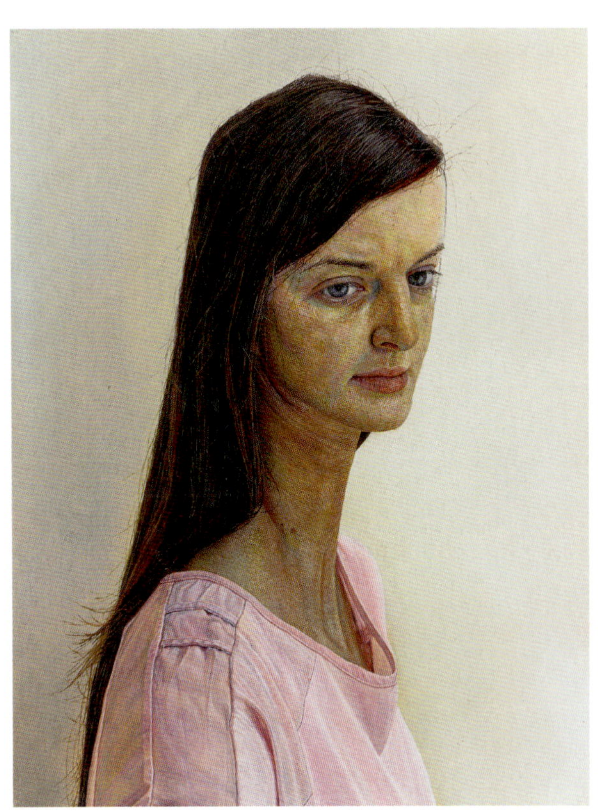

Girl without Pearl Earring
Bas Nijenhuis

Oil on panel
450 × 350mm

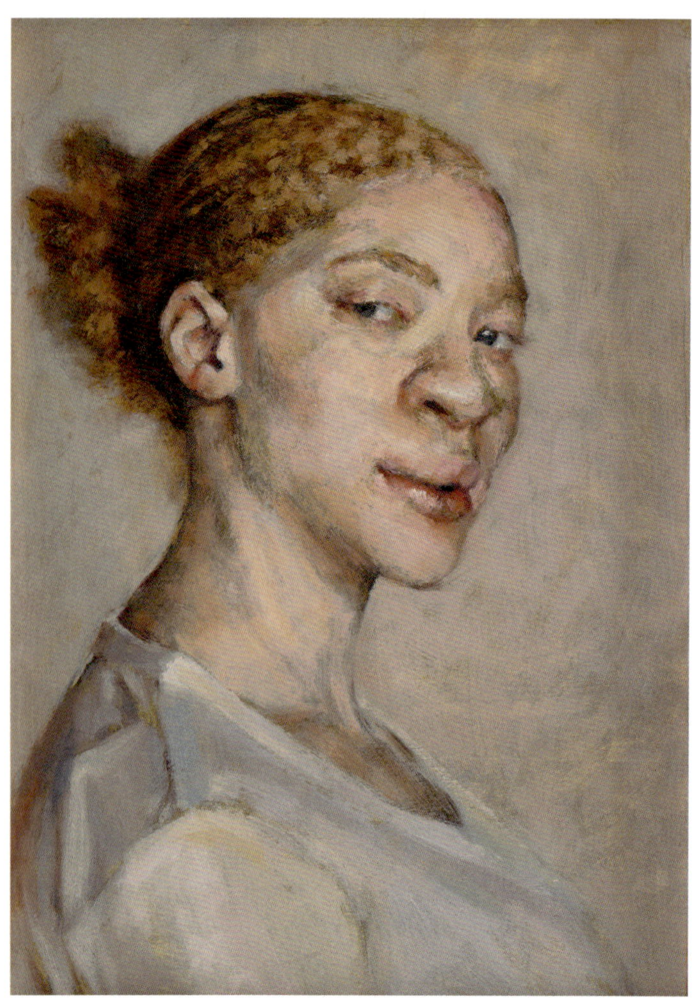

Stephanie
Britta Noresten

Oil on linen
400 × 360mm

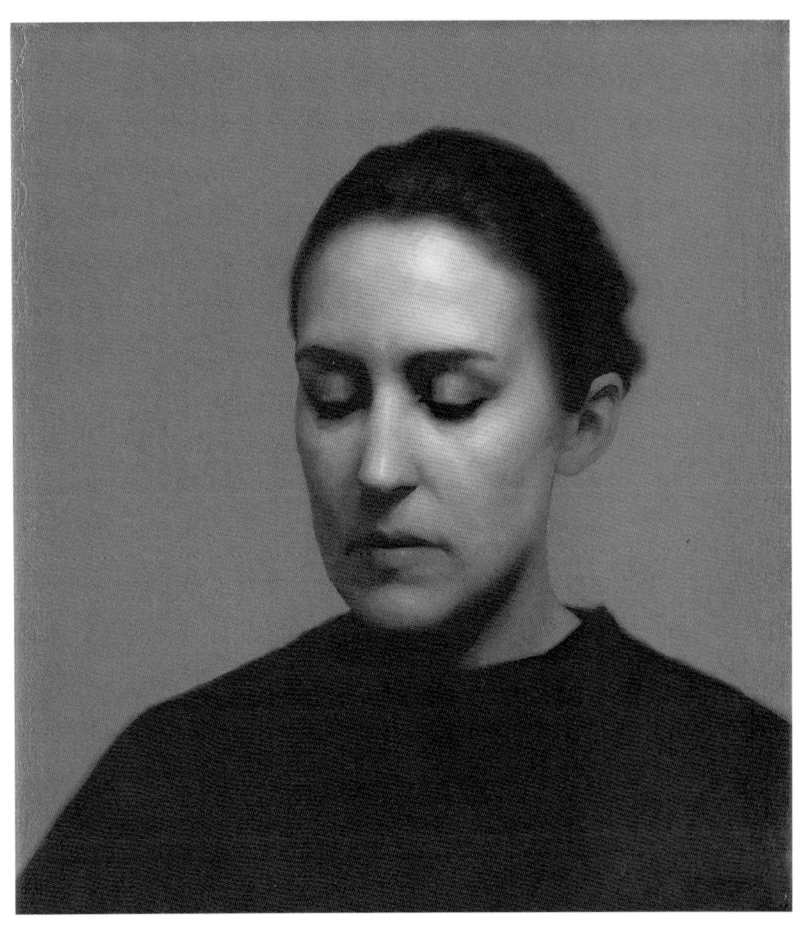

Oil on linen
1200 × 900mm

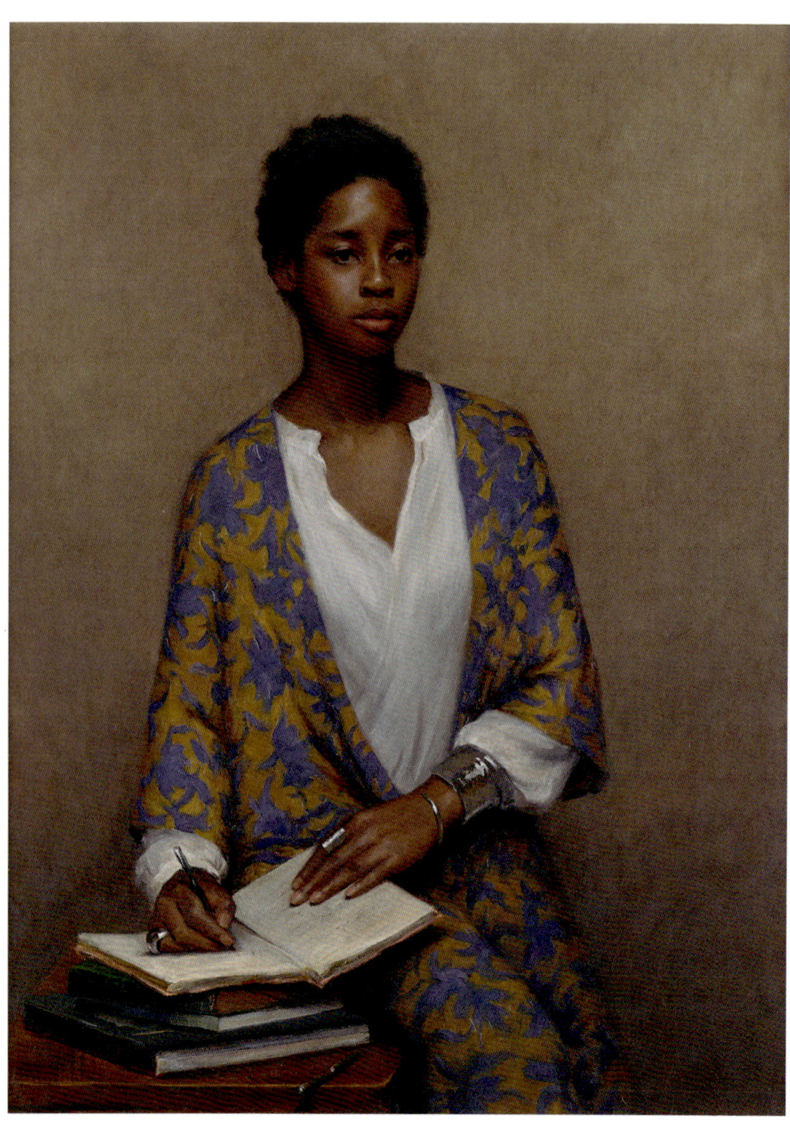

Ninety Years
Miguel Angel Oyarbide

Oil on panel
1000 × 675mm

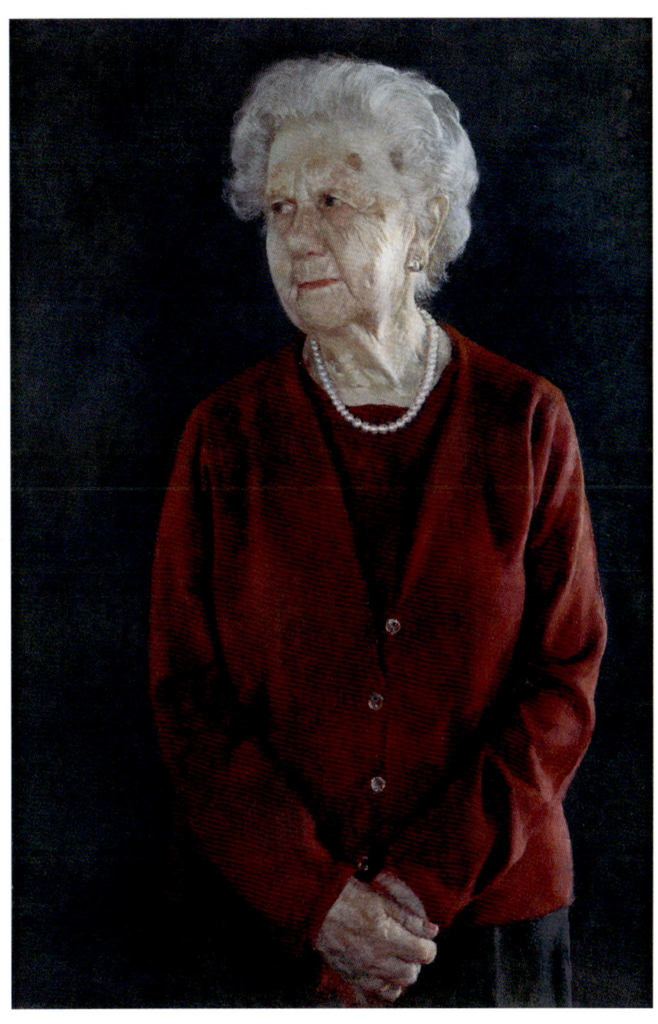

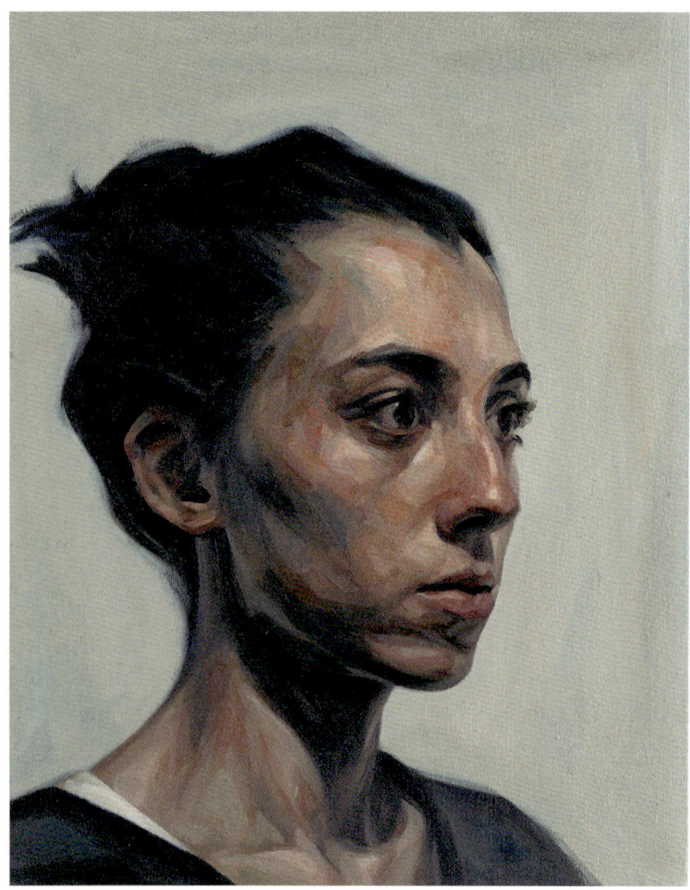

Resting
Helen Lee Robinson

Oil on board
550 × 450mm

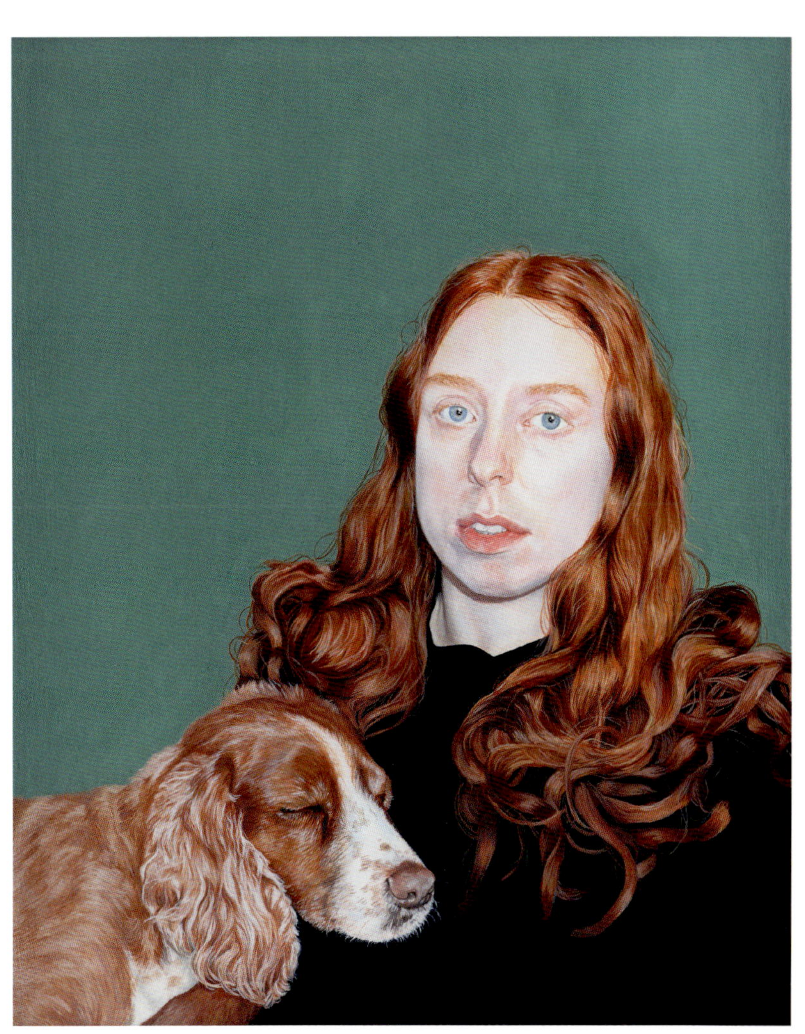

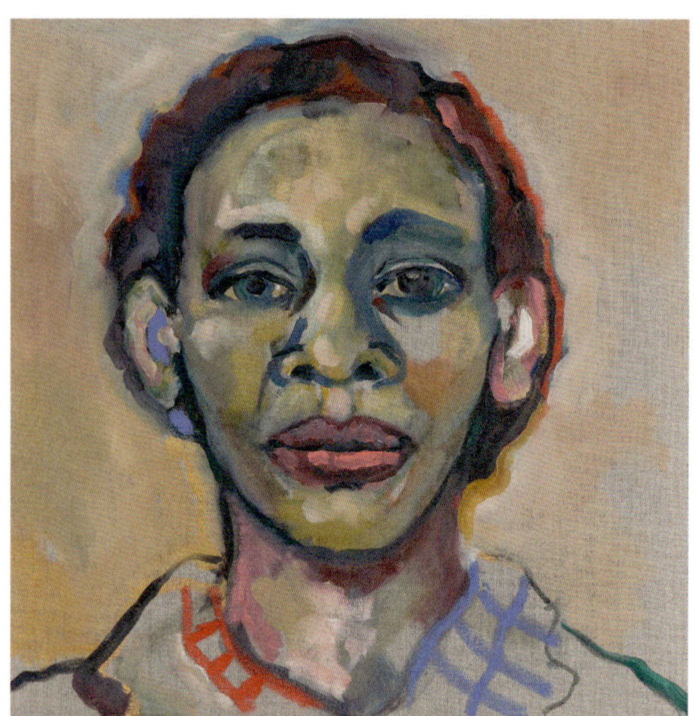

Jenne
Manu Kaur Saluja

Oil on linen
910 × 910mm

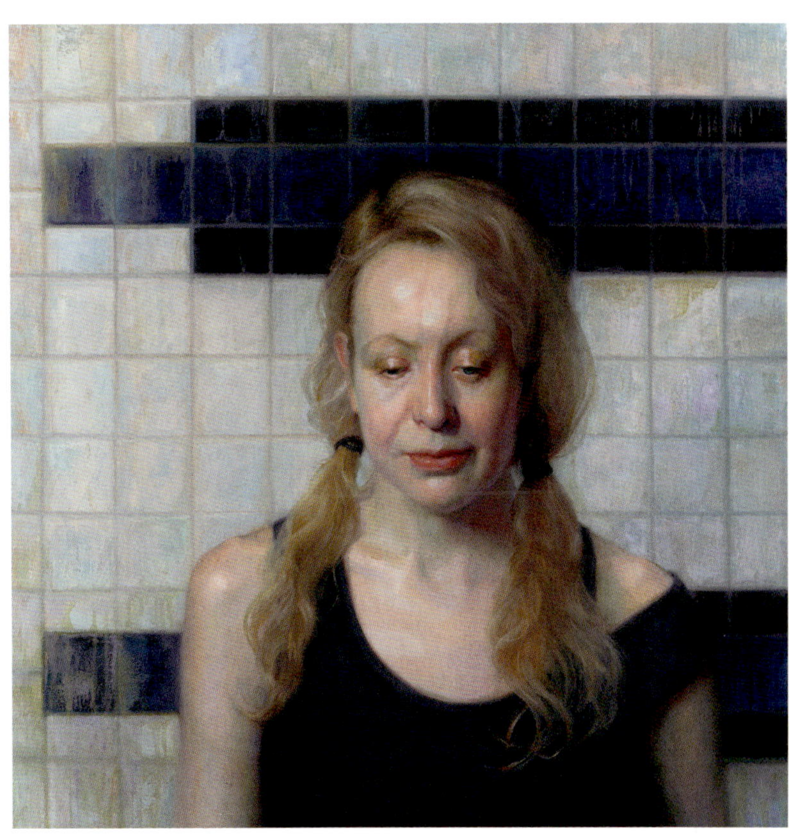

Oil on canvas
1000 × 700mm

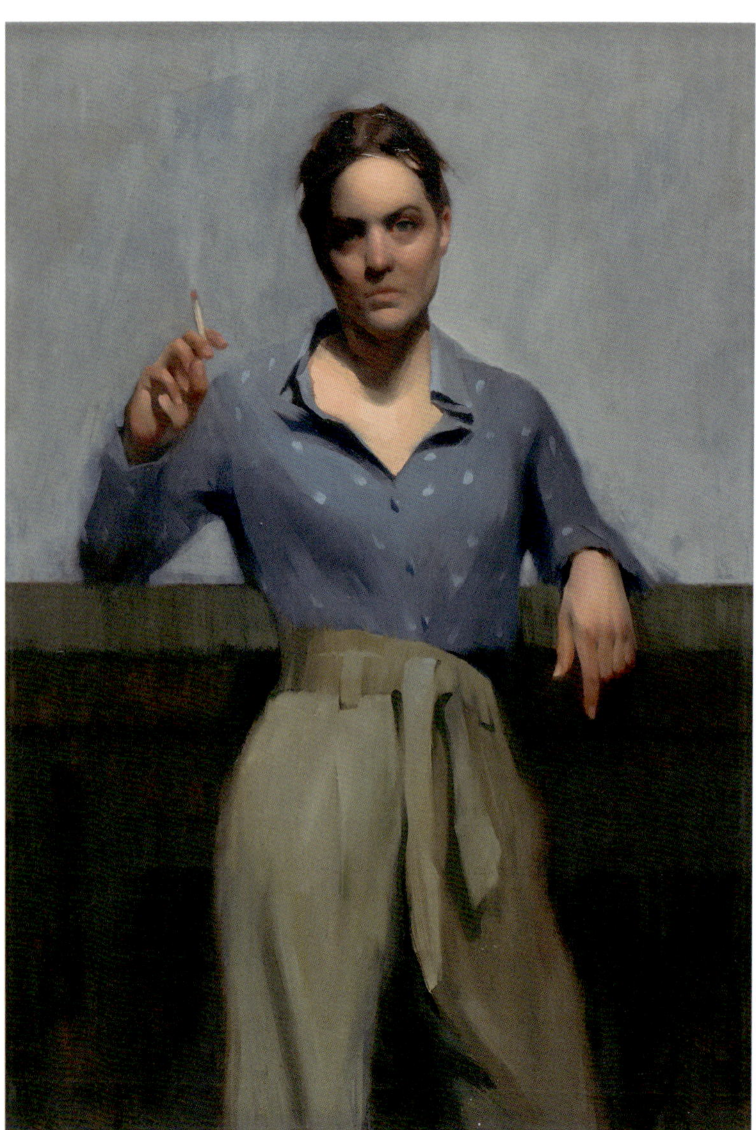

Young Girl
Elaine Speirs
Oil on board
770 × 1000mm

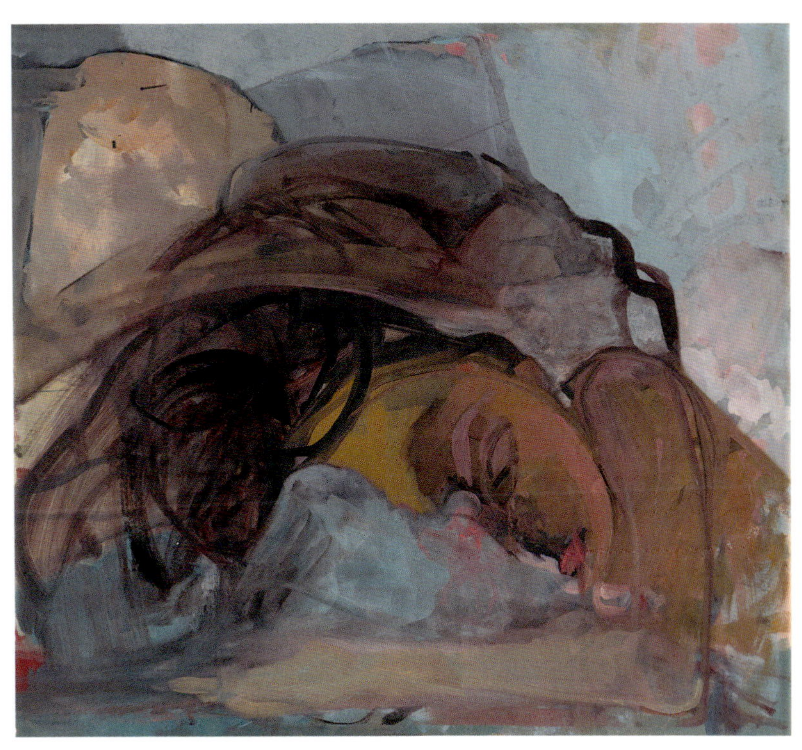

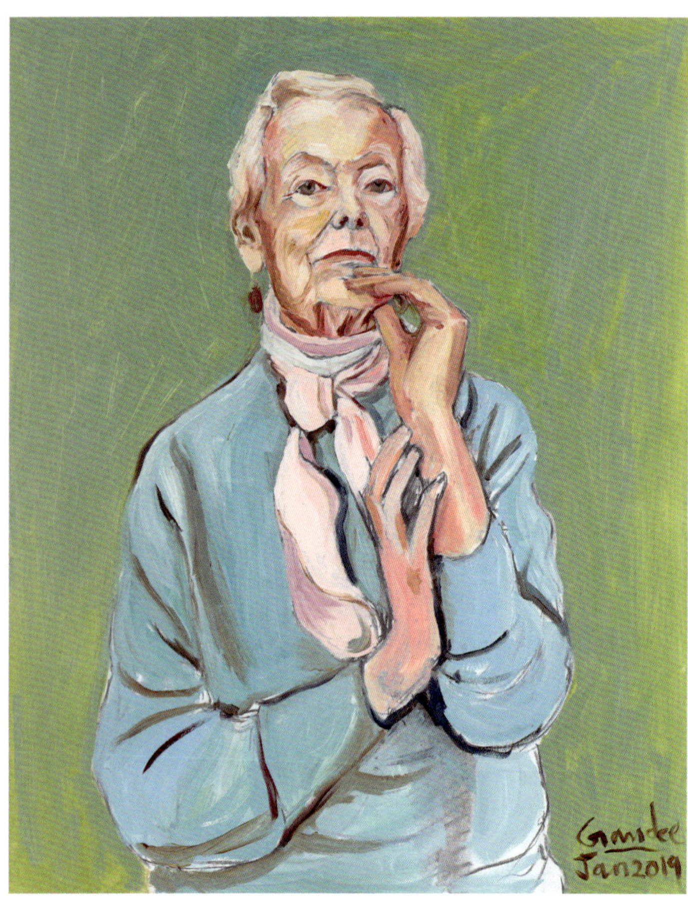

Davetta
Natalie Voelker

Oil on canvas
1520 × 1220mm

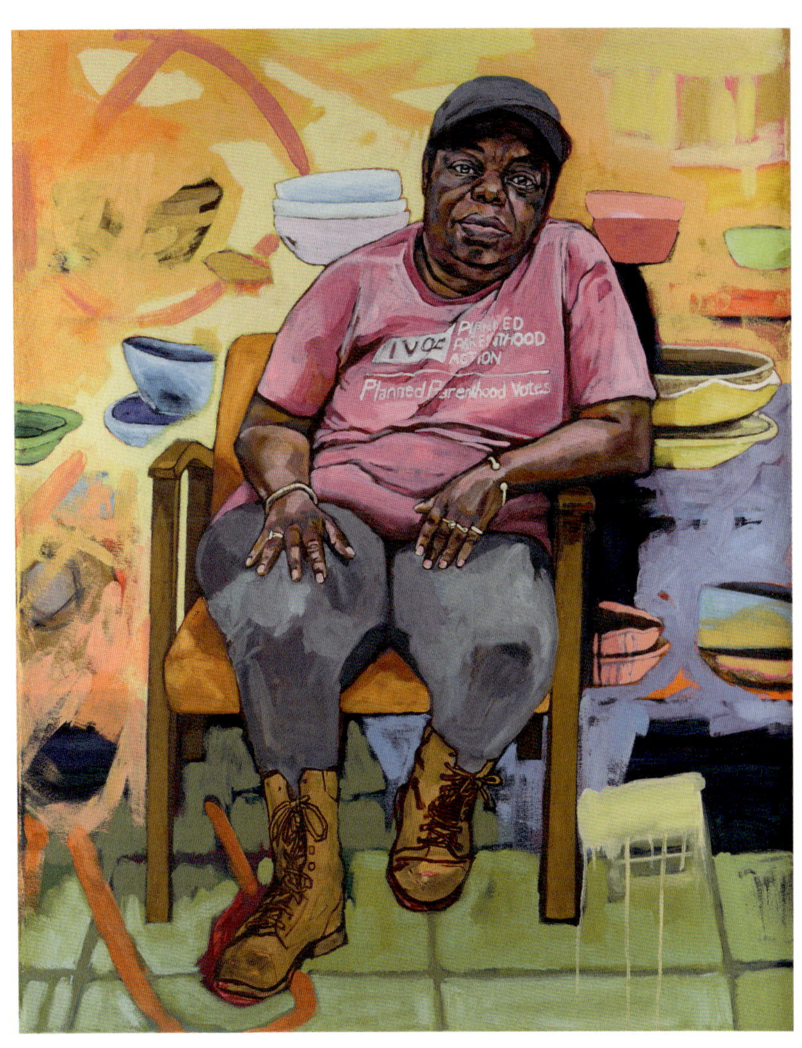

Mixed media (compressed charcoal,
acrylic paint and lacquer)
1290 × 1570mm

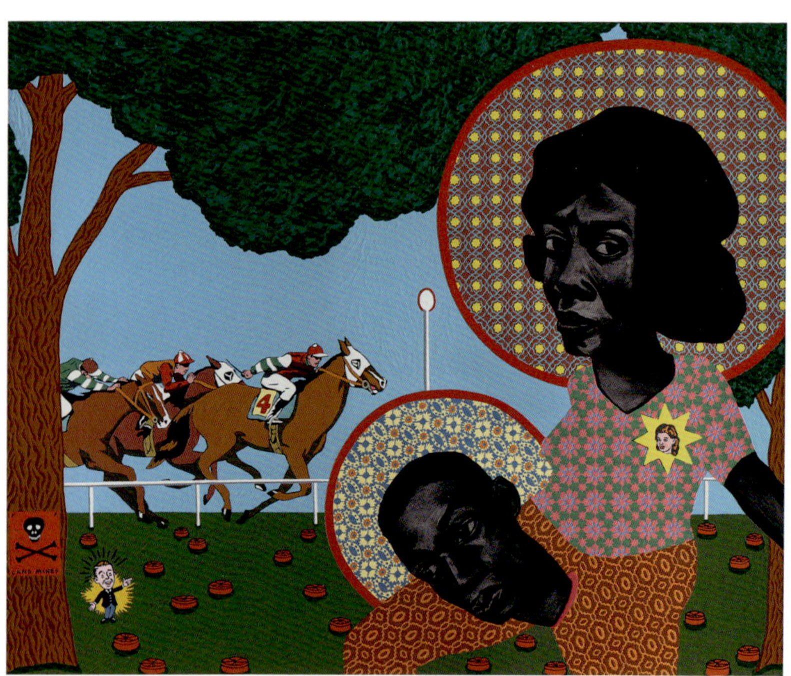

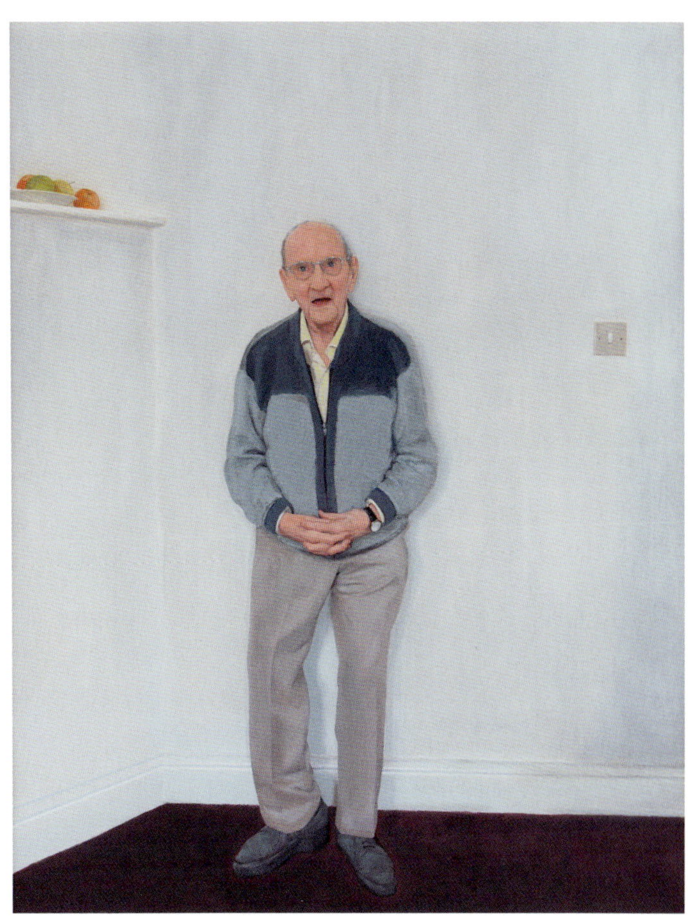

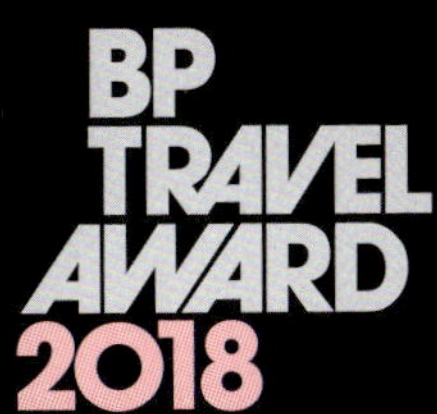

Each year exhibitors are invited to submit a proposal for the BP Travel Award. The aim of this award is to give an artist the opportunity to experience working in a different environment in Britain or abroad, and on a project related to portraiture. The artist's work is then shown as part of the following year's BP Portrait Award exhibition and tour.

THE JUDGES

Rosie Broadley
Collections Curator,
National Portrait Gallery

Benjamin Sullivan
Artist and winner of
2017 BP Portrait Award

Des Violaris
Director, UK Arts & Culture, BP

Tony Wheeler
Co-Founder, Lonely Planet

The Prizewinner 2018
Robert Seidel, who received £8,000 for his proposal to cycle through eight different countries along the Danube River and create portraits along the way.

BP TRAVEL AWARD 2018 INTRODUCTION

The National Portrait Gallery's BP Portrait Award 2018 featured forty-eight selected paintings, but as well as First, Second and Third Prizes and a Young Artist Award there's also an annual Travel Award. Last year's entries to the Award came in from eighty-eight countries, so there's clearly a lot of travel involved even before the judges make their decisions. The Travel Award is open to any of the exhibiting artists except the four prizewinners, and it helps the winning artist to work in a different environment and then
bring the resulting portraits to the following year's exhibition.

Travelling along the 'hippie trail' across Asia in the early 1970s led to my involvement in the creation of the travel publisher Lonely Planet and, as a result, a lifetime of travel. I'm regularly asked, 'Where's your favourite place?' and the answer is, 'The departure lounge.' It was therefore a delight to be asked to join the panel of judges for the BP Travel Award 2018. The Travel Award has always intrigued me and I was so taken with Carl Randall's Japan portraits from his 2012 Travel Award explorations that I ended up buying some of them. As I write this, I can glance up at the wall to see those favourite portraits gazing back at me.

Now, I am no painter – I know what I like hanging on my walls, but my artistic expertise goes no further than that. My fellow judges for the Travel Award certainly made up for my shortcomings, however for this competition art isn't the only question; travel has to come into it as well. I found myself arguing against proposals that I felt didn't travel enough.

That certainly was not a failing with Robert Seidel's painting travels, as he followed the Danube River from its source in Germany to its mouth on the Black Sea. The Danube covers almost 3000 kilometres and is the second-longest river in Europe. It passes through or borders ten countries, more than any other river in the world.

Tony Wheeler
Co-Founder, Lonely Planet

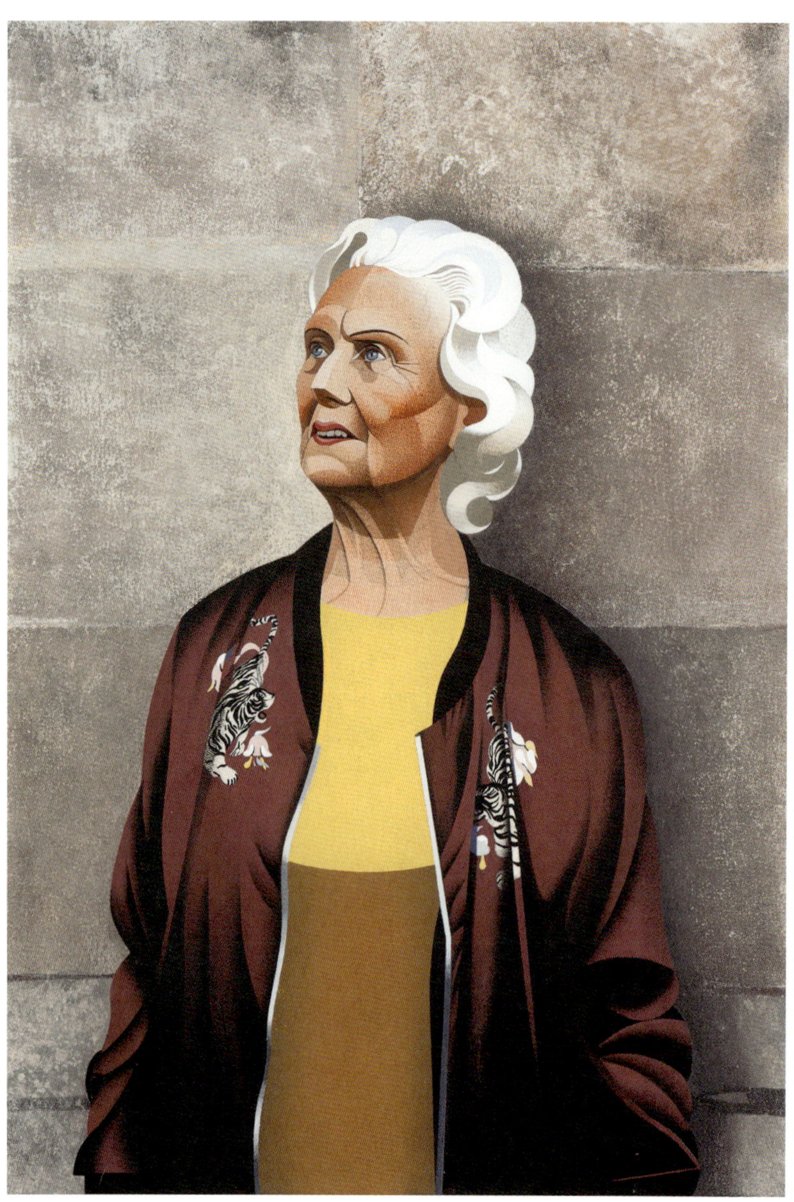

Mary by Robert Seidel, 2019
Egg tempera on canvas, 500 × 350mm

Robert Seidel's winning submission for the BP Travel Award 2018 was not only an ambitious creative project, but a considerable physical challenge at the same time. An avid cyclist, the German artist proposed biking the length of the Danube River, a distance of some 3000 kilometres, painting portraits of people he met along the way.

Flowing southeast from its source in Germany's Black Forest, the Danube is Europe's second-longest river and passes through or borders ten countries and four capital cities (Vienna, Bratislava, Budapest and Belgrade), before reaching Ukraine where it drains into the Black Sea. 'The Danube connects more countries than any other river in the world so it provides a wonderful picture of Europe's plurality and diversity,' says Seidel. 'I wanted to reflect the mood of the people along the river, tell their stories, and capture the most exciting encounters in portraits.'

The artist planned to cycle as much of the route as he could, carrying his materials in two saddlebags, while hopping aboard trains, buses and cruise boats when necessary. He began in the Bavarian town of Donaueschingen, where the Danube rises, and passed 'lush green meadows, heavy fruit trees and stork nests' on his opening stage, which followed a riverside bike trail along the German-Austrian border.

Even torrential rainstorms couldn't dampen his spirits. 'My glasses were fogged and my shoes were soaked like sponges, but I was tense and excited,' he recalls. 'Would my idea work? How would people react to my project?'

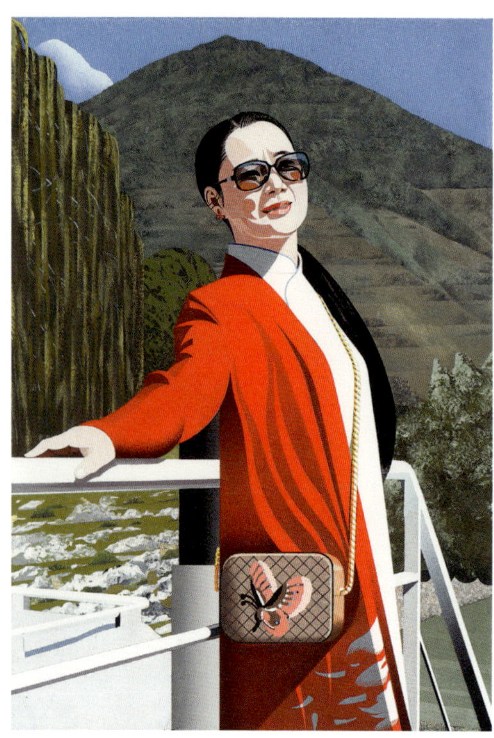

Z Hang Lin by Robert Seidel, 2019
Egg tempera on canvas, 500 × 350mm

Seidel approached potential subjects by handing them a postcard designed by a graphic artist friend, which explained the project in English and featured an example of his work: a portrait of a San Francisco local called David. Seidel had painted the work during an artist residency at the ESMoA gallery in El Segundo, California, and it was displayed in the BP Portrait Award 2018 exhibition.

Inviting local people to pose for his Danube portraits, he also approached some of the tourists sightseeing along the route. Among the first to catch his eye was a Chinese actress, Z Hang Lin, who he noticed aboard a cruise boat in the picturesque Wachau region of Austria where the river flows past monasteries and vineyards. She was visiting Europe with a tour group of fellow actors from Shaoxing. 'I loved her poise, the beautiful backdrop, and the cultural contrast between Austria and China,' says Seidel.

'I wanted to make a portrait, but since no one from the group could

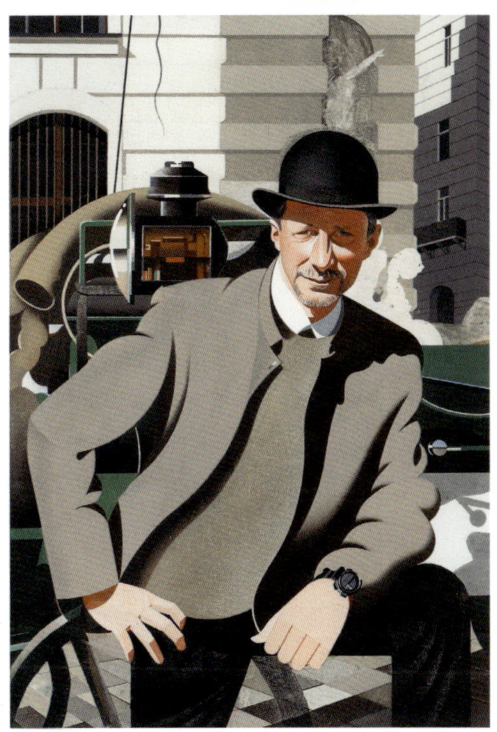

Lazlo by Robert Seidel, 2018
Egg tempera on canvas, 500 × 350mm

speak English, communication
was impossible until a tour guide
managed to help out.'

Wherever possible, Seidel made
sketches and watercolours of his
subjects, though time constraints
meant that he also took photographs
as part of his pre-studio procedure.
'The tight schedule was a defining
feature of the journey. On the road,
I collected and inhaled everything
as completely as I could. Later, in
the studio, was when I classified
and evaluated.'

Austria proved to be fertile territory
for the artist, in particular its 'confident
and eloquent' capital. While in
Vienna, Seidel was drawn to a
'splendid-looking' Hungarian
coachman, Lazlo, standing with his
horse and carriage. Soon after, he
sketched an Irish tourist, Mary, who
was visiting St Stephen's Cathedral.
'Mary's outfit was exciting and
when we got talking there was a
real connection.'

As his journey continued, he spent
less time in the saddle. 'Cycling was

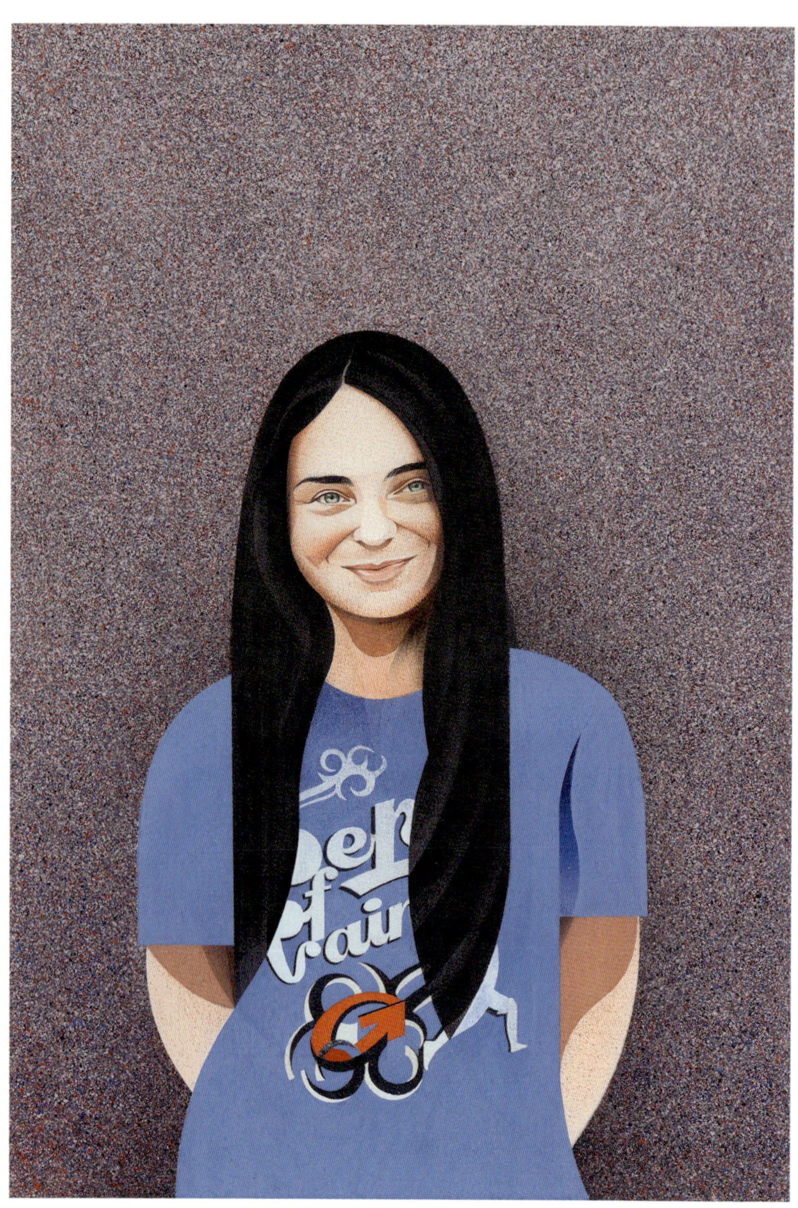

Merina by Robert Seidel, 2019
Egg tempera on canvas, 500 × 350mm

certainly the best means of getting in contact with people and exploring regions, but in Hungary the roads started to get dilapidated and the cars were bigger and faster. I got fed up. It was loud, dirty and dangerous.' Arriving in Budapest by bus, Seidel revived body and soul in the city's thermal baths, but struggled to connect with the locals. 'As a painter who observes from a distance or works alone in the studio, it was unusual for me to address people directly on the street,' he says. 'It got easier as I went on, but it was always a challenge to outline the project and engage with someone at the same time.'

In Romania, time restrictions forced Seidel to reconsider the project and he reluctantly decided to bypass the Danube's final two countries, Moldova and Ukraine. Instead he caught a train from Bucharest to the port of Constanța, following the route of the Danube–Black Sea Canal and pausing to sketch and photograph Florin, a railway worker with a 'melancholic demeanour'. Cycling the short distance from Constanța to the resort of Eforie Nord, Seidel reunited with an artist friend, Julius, who had accompanied him on several earlier stages of the trip. Together they celebrated with

cocktails in the hotel bar before gathering shells from the beach and bathing in the Black Sea to signal the journey's end.

After four weeks on the road, Seidel returned to his studio where he sorted through photographs and sketches of around fifty people, selecting eight subjects to mark the eight countries he visited. 'For the final portraits I chose people who had made a lasting impression on me. It was good to be back in the studio. Ideas happen everywhere, but I need a quiet and structured place to work constructively.'

Born in the town of Grimma, Saxony, in 1983, Seidel currently lives and works in Leipzig after graduating from the city's Hochschule für Grafik und Buchkunst (Academy of Fine Arts Leipzig). Among Seidel's tutors was Neo Rauch, one of the most important German painters of his generation who was a leading figure in the New Leipzig School, the celebrated movement often associated with traditions of draughtsmanship, composition and narrative. 'I definitely feel part of that tradition. I am committed to figurative, narrative painting,' says Seidel. 'The greatest thing I learned from Neo Rauch was attitude.'

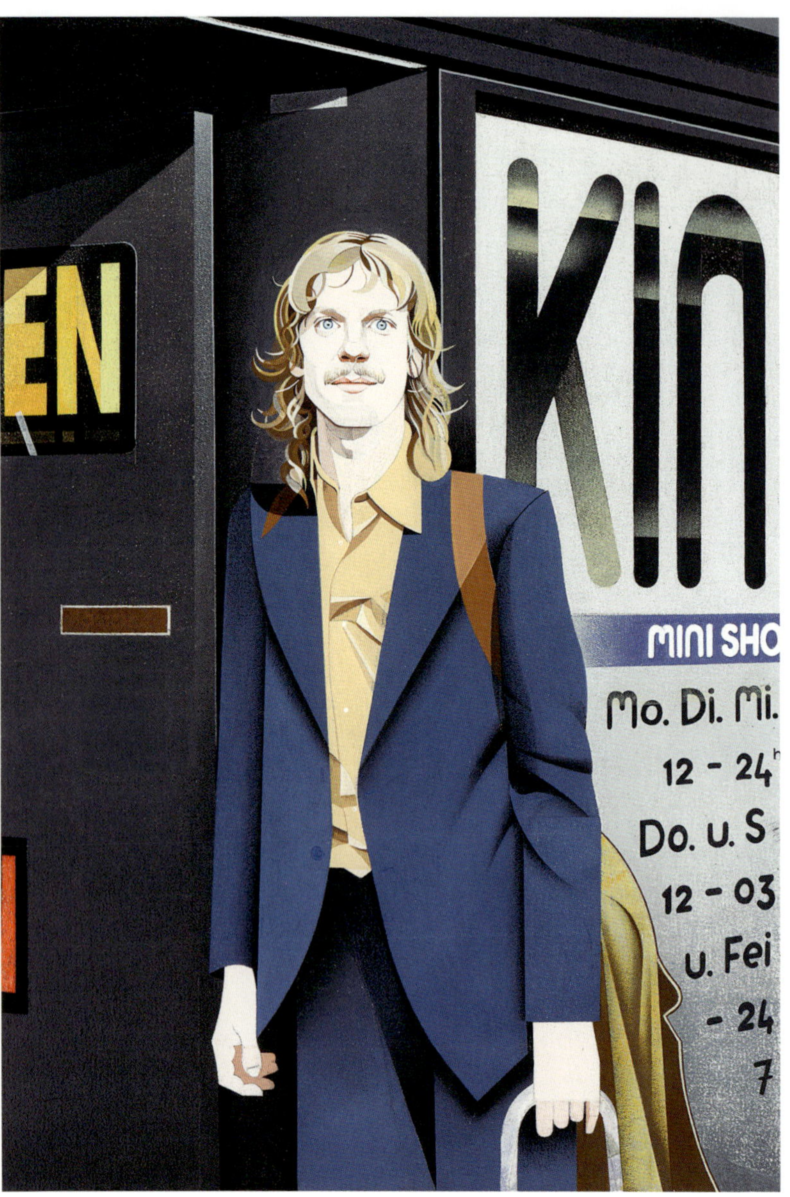

Voodoo Jürgens by Robert Seidel, 2018
Egg tempera on canvas, 500 × 350mm

Until recently, Seidel rarely painted the human form. His most recent exhibitions include a 2016 solo show at the Gerhard Hofland gallery in Amsterdam, which featured a series of large-scale architectural landscapes. In *Colours of Descents*, a 2017 group show at Leipzig's G2 Kunsthalle, he explored the abstract structures of early 1990s video game graphics. 'People have become interesting for me only in the last few years. I … did not dare to approach the topic. I finally opened up to the figure by painting old reggae album covers and I am now open to all subjects of painting.'

Seidel spent around a month on each of his Danube portraits, working in his preferred egg tempera, the centuries-old medium in which pigments are mixed with egg yolk emulsion. 'Egg tempera can create a great tension in the paintings,' he explains. 'I can work glazed and opaque; I can wash the paint down after applying, scrape and polish. I also like the brilliance and brittleness of the colour. For me, a good painting is strangeness paired with a surprising moment. It has to move me and be readable in several ways.' Seidel's travels coincided with continuing political ferment in Europe as the continent grappled with the migrant crisis and a surge in nationalism. However, Seidel deliberately shied away from addressing political issues in the works. 'National pride was a big topic of conversation, especially in Hungary, Croatia and Serbia,' he says. 'But I'm not interested in making statements. I wanted to travel with open eyes and discover what is driving European society today beyond abstract political ideas and recent crises. By painting, I examine objects and relationships in order to form my own impression.'

The Danube portraits, he believes, are a positive reflection of the cultural diversity and 'different life concepts' still to be found across Europe despite increasing globalisation. 'My paintings are a kaleidoscope of today's society,' he says. 'The Danube is fundamental and romantic, and I took the idiosyncrasy of the river as a model. I found the variety, the different landscapes and cultural backgrounds very appealing, and it was satisfying to venture out of my comfort zone.'

Interview by Richard McClure

BP PORTRAIT AWARD: PREVIOUS PRIZEWINNERS

Over the years, the BP Portrait Award has served to extend the art of portraiture. In the interviews that follow, three former prizewinners reflect on their experience of the competition and on the works that won them First Prize. Two of the artists – Ishbel Myerscough, who was award First Prize in 1995, and Stuart Pearson Wright, who won First Prize in 2001 – are now well-represented in the Gallery's collection, while the third, Clara Drummond, has yet to embark on the commission that came with winning the First Prize in 2016. They each offer a unique perspective on what winning the Award has meant to them.

PREVIOUS PRIZEWINNERS

Ishbel Myerscough
BP Portrait Award 1995

Stuart Pearson Wright
BP Portrait Award 2001

Clara Drummond
BP Portrait Award 2016

Krishenda
Ishbel Myerscough, 1995

Oil on canvas
860 × 1840mm

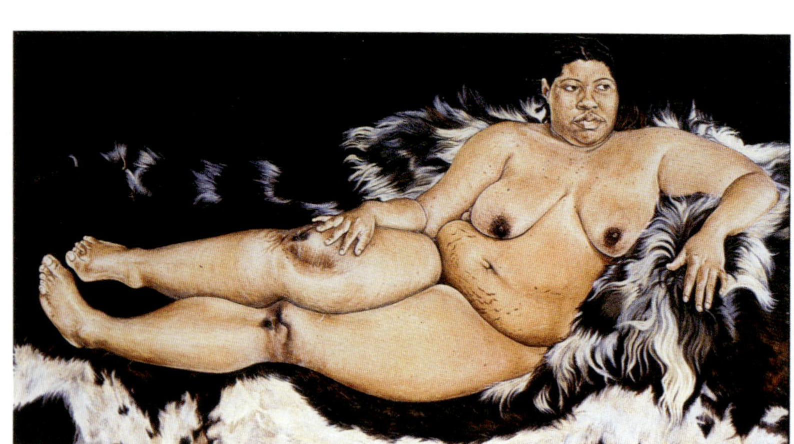

Ishbel Myerscough's approach to the human figure has changed little since she first took up the subject in the early 1990s. It was as a student at the Glasgow School of Art that she started entering works into the competition, taking encouragement from Glasgow alumni who had gone on to win prizes, such as Alison Watt who was awarded First Prize in 1987. These early submissions comprised self-portraits and studies of close friends, and attracted attention for the artist's intense, almost forensic, scrutiny of her subjects and her honesty in accepting the body for what it is regardless of what the sitter might desire it to be.

Myerscough's models are often described as looking older than their actual age at the time of painting, an aspect that relates to her slow method of working (the average portrait takes three months) and her clear, hard-edged style with figures isolated against a plain background. She is particularly interested in skin, which she describes as 'a layer of many colours' that is compelling to behold while also communicating mutability and the idea of individual existence frozen in time. Such characteristics are typical of the northern European artists she identifies with, from Lucas Cranach to Lucian Freud in more recent times.

Although she prefers to work from life, observing her subjects over a long period of time, she also uses photographs of isolated fragments to zone in on a particular area, such as an ear or eye. This approach is consistent with her practice of manipulating what she sees in order to capture what it feels like to inhabit a body, be it her own or that of another person in her life.

Myerscough had three works accepted for the BP Award exhibition (two of which were commended and one of which won Third Prize) before she emerged as the outright winner in 1995 with her challenging portrait *Krishenda*. Fearing it would be rejected, she entered the portrait just an hour before the deadline. The painting is a bold and uncompromising depiction of a woman reclining on a goat skin rug proudly brandishing the stretch marks and bruises on her body. 'The sitter was an American model who had endless men running after her', Myerscough recalls, 'and I found her fascinating. I could not see her pubic area because of her flesh but that did not in any way diminish her beauty. The reality of her became my vision.'

Krishenda proved to be significant at a time when a number of artists projected flesh as an aesthetic, as also seen in the figurative work of Jenny Saville. As for the Award, Myerscough feels it is difficult for artists to stand out in the same way today and, having since been a competition judge, believes there is a fine line between verisimilitude and the creation of meaning in art.

Interview by Alison Smith

Gallus Gallus with Still Life and Presidents
Stuart Pearson Wright, 2001

Oil on linen
1915 × 1715mm

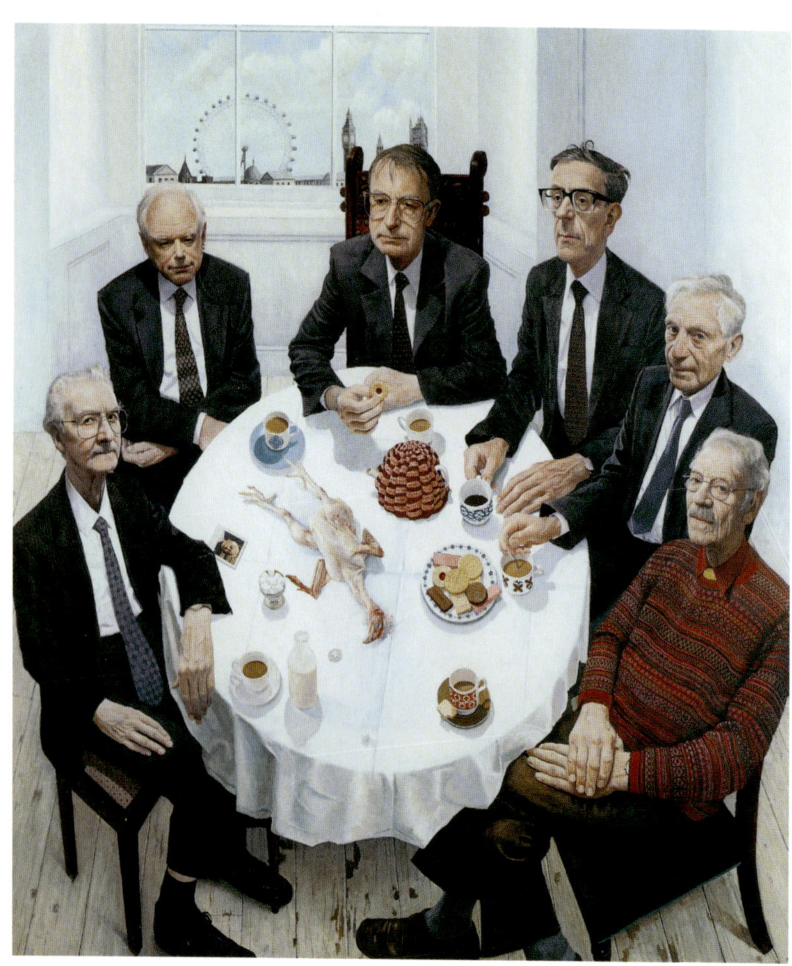

Stuart Pearson Wright describes himself as a painter who makes portraits rather than a portrait painter per se. He is interested in role play, or the transition between real and assumed identity, and is particularly drawn to actors, having worked in theatre. Like them, he looks for something in a character he can connect with, which further explains the strong element of self-projection in his work – the elongated faces and melancholy aura that disclose something of the artist's own appearance and perspective on the world.

Pearson Wright first became interested in portraiture as a child and recalls being struck by *The Somerset House Conference, 1604* on a visit to the National Portrait Gallery. He was intrigued by the tilted perspective of the table and the way it appears to shift as the eye moves from head to head. It was with this image in mind that he later painted *Gallus Gallus with Still Life and Presidents*, a commission from the British Academy to be placed above a fireplace in a waiting room in its London headquarters.

Designed to be looked at from below, this all-male group portrait plays with shape in a similar way to the Somerset House picture, but here the circular forms of the London Eye and table double up as a wheel of fortune motif. The shocking placement of a plucked, dead chicken on the table, seemingly inappropriate for a gathering of distinguished scholars, lends the image a grotesque 'Neue Sachlichkeit' quality while also being comic. The artist remembers the academicians' astonishment when the painting was unveiled: 'As the curtain fell back, their eyes literally revolved around the picture; alighting on the table, they all frowned and stared with disbelief at the chicken.'

Surprised that they did not grasp the visual meaning or humour of the painting, Pearson Wright decided to test it on a broader audience by submitting the picture to the 2001 BP Portrait Award where it won First Prize. During interviews when his prizewinning work was revealed, he found himself later portrayed as a defender of artists who worked in traditional styles as opposed to the more conceptual art championed by many modern and contemporary art institutions and galleries.

Since winning the Award, Pearson Wright feels he has worked between being a society painter and a contemporary artist and has experienced enough success to have been able to pursue his own interests. His 'mini-theatre' portrait of the novelist J.K. Rowling, the commission that followed on from the prize, is one of the most popular works in the Gallery's collection and his portraits of actors were the focus of the 2006 display *Most People are Other People*, also shown at the Gallery.

Interview by Alison Smith

Girl in a Liberty Dress
Clara Drummond, 2016

Oil on board
260 × 370mm

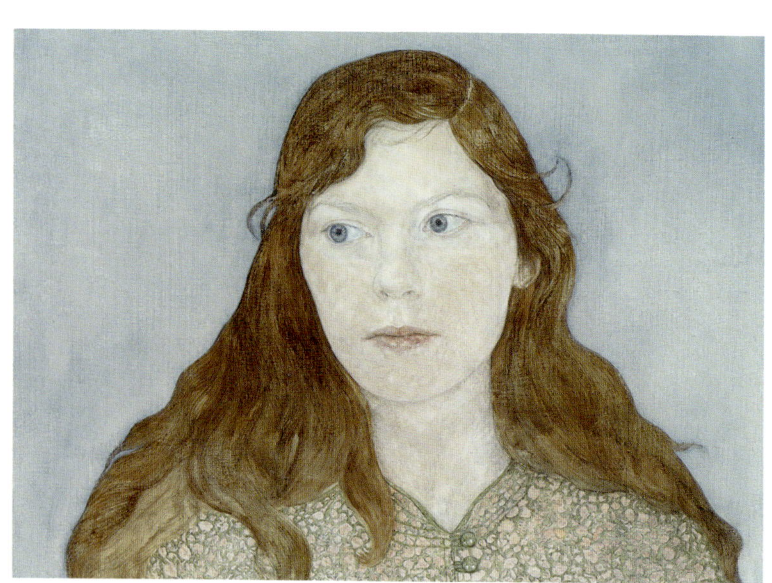

Girl in a Liberty Dress
Clara Drummond, 2016

Oil on board
260 × 370mm

Although Clara Drummond always wanted to be a painter, her route to becoming one was by no means conventional. After studying modern languages at Cambridge University, she worked as a part-time assistant to the artist Jonathan Yeo before undertaking a Master's degree at The Prince's Drawing School (now The Royal Drawing School). The experience of posing for and painting other students came as a revelation, encouraging the collaborative approach she has abided by ever since. Over a period of several years she focused on representing fellow-artist Kirsty Buchanan, with whom she shares a deep interest in women's history, and had two portraits of her accepted for the BP Portrait Award exhibition before winning First Prize in 2016 with *Girl in a Liberty Dress*.

This painting was based on a drawing of Buchanan wearing a vintage Liberty dress, a sign of both artists' admiration for the design work of Jane and May Morris, which they were researching as part of a project for the William Morris Society archive. Employing a palette of earth colours (Drummond only uses five pigments), the artist reworked the portrait from memory using a thin layer of paint and then wiping off the black background to expose the underlying white priming. This swift technique contrasts with the more delicate treatment of the dress with its 'sea anemone' flowers and the figure's treacle-like hair, the colour of which was dictated by the look and feel of the medium rather than by any desire to be true to the sitter herself; neither the artist nor subject has red hair. 'It was not my intention to make the portrait look real,' she maintains. 'In fact, the end result could be said to look more like me than Kirsty.'

The picture has a quiet and enigmatic quality, as if conveying the idea of a conversation or the mutual understanding between the two women. At the time that Drummond was painting Buchanan, both artists were set on challenging the idea of the artist's muse as epitomised by both the romantic art of the Pre-Raphaelites and the uncomfortable realism of Lucian Freud. 'A muse can be a catalyst for creativity, not just someone who serves it,' she affirms. Freud has been an important influence on Drummond and while she admires his honesty of observation she believes there is a voracious quality to his art especially when it comes to female sitters: 'He looks with an intensity that borders on the alarming – like a hawk about to devour a mouse.'

Drummond's initial reaction on winning the First Prize was to feel overwhelmed, as if undeserving of the limelight. 'I now feel I won it for others – to tell those painters working like myself in isolation not to be so self-effacing. For me the Portrait Award has played a vital role in giving the aspiring artist a voice.'

Interview by Alison Smith

ACKNOWLEDGEMENTS

My congratulations are offered to all the artists in the exhibition and especially to the prizewinners, Charlie Schaffer, Carl-Martin Sandvold and Massimiliano Pironti, and to Emma Hopkins, the winner of the prize for a younger painter. I would also like to thank all the artists who decided to enter the 2019 competition.

I would like to thank my fellow judges: Gaylene Gould, Gary Hume, Alison Smith, Des Violaris and Zoé Whitley. Their dedication and observations throughout the judging process were invaluable and it was a pleasure to work with them all. I would also like to thank the judges of the BP Travel Award 2019: Miriam Escofet, Alison Smith and Des Violaris. I am very grateful to Christopher Baker for his engaging essay for the catalogue. My thanks to Kara Green, Richard McClure and Tijana Todorinovic for their editorial work, Richard Ardagh Studio for designing the catalogue, and to Clementine Williamson for her overall management of the 2019 BP Portrait Award, ably assisted by Claire Floyd. Many other colleagues at the National Portrait Gallery have been involved in making the competition and exhibition a continued success and my thanks for their hard work go to Janet Alexander, Pim Baxter, Miranda Banfield, Natalia Calvocoressi, Andrea Easey, Evie Hone, Jessie Hunt, Jessica Litwin, Laura McKechan, Ruth Müller-Wirth, Juno Rae, Jude Simmons, Fiona Smith, Liz Smith, Emelia Spofforth-Jones, Anna Starling, Sarah Tinsley, Ben Weaver, Helen Whiteoak, Rosie Wilson, and Karl Lydon and the art handling team. Many thanks to The White Wall Company for their contribution to the efficient management of the selection and judging process.

Nicholas Cullinan
Director, National Portrait Gallery

Picture Credits
All works © the Artist, except for pages 10, 16 and 19 © National Portrait Gallery, London; page 11 © National Galleries of Scotland; pages 78, 80–2, 84 © Robert Seidel, Photography: Sebastian Komnick.

The publisher would like to thank the copyright holders for granting permission to reproduce works illustrated in this book. Every effort has been made to contact the holders of copyright material and any omissions will be corrected in future editions if the publisher is notified in writing.

INDEX